# "GOD SEND FRIDAY"

## Autobiography
## of a Dublin Seafarer

### Jim Purdy

GLENDALE

First published in Ireland 1991
by Glendale Publishing Ltd.
1 Summerhill Parade
Sandycove
Co. Dublin

**British Library Cataloguing in Publication Data**
Purdy, Jim
   God send Friday:  autobiography of a Dublin seafarer.
   1.  Shipping : Merchant Ships
   I.   Title
   387.5092

   ISBN 0–907606–90–3

Origination by Wendy A. Commins
The Curragh, Co. Kildare
Printed by Colour Books, Dublin

*For Lydia*
*with thanks for the*
*better days*

# Prologue

After many lonely nights in the twenty years of my life spent as a seafarer, with times my only solace being the comfort of a book, I can say that reading books gave me pleasure, great pleasure. The escapism I discovered while wedged in my bunk braving a North Atlantic storm, or resting on a day-bed naked, sweating while the ship cut through the calm and warm nights of the tropics, established in me a taste for biography above all other kinds of book — biography and memoirs.

I have read many biographies — written by the famous and wealthy but by modest people too, gardeners, chauffeurs and the like — all had one common stamp, a vast experience of life. They had lived life and recorded their living. Some were destined to remain famous, others faded into obscurity. If there were winners I like to think the laurels would go to those who had to struggle most, the apparent non-starters in life's race who were destined to travel uphill from the beginning, uphill from poverty, lack of educational opportunity, hard times. I would say that naturally because that's where I myself came from.

I have heard it said there is a book in everyone. Well I now take my chance, with modest ambition and with gratitude for my years of extracting pleasure and knowledge from other writers' efforts.

If a man has the temerity to write the story of his life. He should have a double aim: First to show it and his little ego in relation to the time and place in which he lived his life, to the procession of historical events, even to the absurd metaphysics of The Universe.

Secondly, to describe as simply as he can his personal life, not to history and The Universe, but to persons and himself. His record in the trivial, difficult, fascinating art of living from day to day, hour by hour, minute by minute.

*Downhill All The Way*, Leonard Woolf

A reaping of words
A harvest of time
Through inclement weather
It's all here together.

Jim Purdy

# Chapter 1

I was born in the Dublin suburb of Sandymount, not a stone's throw or even a shout, from the roar of Ireland's home of rugby, Landsdowne Road; or for that matter, the aptly named Beggers Bush Army Barracks, where many summary executions were perpetrated in the name of Ireland and Freedom. The year was 1934, the street was named Bath Avenue. (Why, oh why, with outside toilets shared with so many?) The 'bath' was a portable affair invariably placed in front of a fire for what would eventually be eleven children. The grand total, including my parents, would be thirteen — unlucky for some.

In 1926 my father, Peter Purdy, a shipwright by trade had married my mother, a local beauty from the nearby small, close-knit, seafaring community called Ringsend.

I don't remember much about Sandymount except, it appears, at one time I tried to escape from my environment by climbing over the side of the pram and falling heavily on my head. I was rushed to the nearest hospital, Sir Patrick Dun's, where eighteen stitches were inserted in my forehead. To this day, my discharge book reads, under distinguishing marks 'Slight scar over left eye'. I was a sickly child and for years I was anaemic. That this was due to the loss of blood at the time of my mishap is pure conjecture. However, if I was indeed trying to escape from Sandymount, I could have saved my parents a lot of heartache because the whole family moved to a new housing complex called Crumlin in 1936. The scheme was engineered by the Dublin Corporation, and most of it was still under construction. My parents were lucky to get one of the first to be completed.

Crumlin is situated south of the city, and lies at the foot of the

Dublin mountains where, in later years, I spent many a happy weekend hiking and camping. Our new house sported a modern indoor bath and toilet — such luxury! At least for the older members of the family, trees of promise from the Irish Free State Government seemed to be bearing fruit. There was an air of gaiety and conciliation for families moving out of Dublin's notorious slums, where tuberculosis and fever seemed to lurk in every corner. Here in Crumlin it was fresh mountain air. Scintilating was a word unheard of then — 'Jaysus, it's grand' was more the norm. It didn't take many years before this orchard bore bad fruit. Soon, out of all these new and luxurious surroundings, emerged a population explosion unprecedented in Irish history since the Great Famine of 1845. By the late 1930s and early 40s, while living in these two-bedroomed houses, the mirror cracked for me and for many more. I was now at an age of awareness and want. Fortunately for all of the family, we had a father who didn't drink. In fact, he went through his whole life without touching a drop. He died in 1974.

Curious, because he spent his whole life working for a brewery, 'Arthur Guinness'. This marvellous company played a major part in our everyday existence. My father tended the barges and the cross-channel ships which transported the black frothy, foaming 'stout', to Liverpool for distribution to various parts of the UK. It was a sad day for Dublin when those barges, which daily tut-tutted up and down the River Liffey, were swept aside by the march of time and progress. Guinness's brewery with its free hospital treatment for employees, dispensary for out-patients and free milk for the needy, was a major factor in our survival to adulthood, and let's face it, we were all in need with only Da's money coming in each Friday.

It was a hard slog for my mother, who had to eke it out. Bread was the staple diet, a loaf which for reasons known to others was called 'a turnover'. Three 'cuts' of bread, as they were known (never slices) were doled out by my father each evening with a 'sup' of tea (never cup) at approximately six o'clock — that was the final meal of the day. The teapot was boiled on the hob, on the grate of a turf-burning fire during the week when we had no pennies for the gas meter. The crust across the top of the bread was called 'the heel' and eagerly sought-after, because this could be nibbled and chewed for ages. Breakfast consisted of two slices of fried bread; dinner was Irish stew — mostly from the soup kitchen. These kitchens existed in most built-up areas and were government sponsored. One queued with a pot or jug, with perhaps threepence, sixpence, or a shilling, depending upon one's funds and needs. My mother added an Oxo cube or two, which added immensely to the flavour. Such was the eternal state of affairs for the weekly Monday to Friday menu. Friday brought a feeling of euphoria, being pay day for most people; that is if you were lucky enough to be working. In our house, anyway, it gave us a feeling of well-being. Da would come home with money and some desperately needed groceries, and all this with a little something for each of us — starting with Ma, a bar of Toblerone chocolate, and for us kids a penny Honeybee bar — a long finger of toffee, which tasted delicious. We would snuggle down by the ample turf fire, to lick and chew the weekly treat with relish having devoured the three cuts of bread and secure in the knowledge that the world was a rosy and contented place. Mouth watering discussions of boxes of chocolates and Honeybee bars would take place: 'When I grow up I'll buy a whole boxful.' And so it would go on: the dreams — our only survival kit.

Saturday and Sunday were different. There was always more to eat. My Da's suit was redeemed from the pawn — sausage and pudding for dinner, with bread and butter, an excellent and tasty meal. Da's only self-indulgence was Saturday afternoon spent at the bookie's. I don't know how much pocket money he kept from his wages. I'd guess about seven shillings. The betting shops, in those far off days, were dingy affairs, although perfectly legal. One could never tell whether my father won or lost; either way, it wouldn't be much. His other vice, if you could call it that, was smoking. Every Saturday — and Saturday *only* — he treated himself to a packet of ten Goldflake cigarettes. They entered his mouth, one after the other, always lighting the following one from the previous one, till the last one emerged from the packet.

Sunday of course was a holy day of obligation to be observed under threat of mortal sin, not to mention the red hot embers of Hell. One took one's arse to Mass with a last minute check from Ma — behind the ears got very close scrutiny. If they were clean and accompanied by a clean shirt collar, off you went to make your peace with God for the coming week. Dinner was different too. Always a roast joint of beef, mushy peas and roast potatoes and mash, followed by jelly and custard — always that. Sunday evening brought mouth watering home-made cake — that never varied. Sunday was always welcome.

Monday dawned all too soon. My Da's suit would be pledged again and the long grind to the following Friday would begin. Crises often loomed, especially when my Da's suit didn't fetch the usual amount from the pawnbroker. This didn't occur often because he only wore it for Mass on Sundays — except when a relative died. Being Catholic, we had our fair share of relatives. Chaos ensued — the reason being my Da's suit had to be redeemed, with a day off work without pay: memories best forgotten.

The first-born in the family was a girl, Margaret. Then came four boys — Jack, Brian, Liam and myself, Jim. Another girl followed, Ursula, then Austin, then twins — a boy and a girl — Dermot and Muriel, followed by another boy, Peter, called after my Da. The last was a girl, Geraldine.

# Chapter 2

My period in school was, in a nutshell, very unhappy and very uneducational. The rigours were first felt at a nun's convent situated in a very run-down part of the city, on the south side, Weaver Square.

As I said, I was a sickly child. I was already dependent on the Guinness dispensary for out-patient treatment: a bottle of iron medicine once a week, two tablespoons daily of the foul smelling concoction was the dosage prescribed. Between that and having stone bruises lanced at regular intervals from the soles of my feet (lack of shoes was the main cause of this trouble), assured me of a regular place in the large Guinness filing cabinet.

I don't remember much about the convent in Weaver Square, except having to bring another pupil home one day, the problem being he'd shit himself. It ran down his legs from under the short trousers which he wore — they were the fashion of the day. We walked home through the streets, he in tears and me sauntering at a respectable distance behind. In fact, I felt somewhat embarrassed. A kindly woman who was walking towards us stopped and asked the reason for his loud and consistent wails. She didn't have the grandstand view from the rear which I had. Needless to say, she was quick to grasp the delicate situation. I noticed her nose twitched distastefully, though she didn't let on.

'Oh, you spilt cocoa on your legs I see', she said.

I tried to be helpful. 'No missus, he's clicked himself'. ('Click' was the polite word for 'Crap').

'There, there, dear child,' she said, handing him a threepenny bit before hurrying away.

The smell quickly left my nostrils. I could envisage cakes and sweets and I moved swiftly to place a protective arm around his shoulders. His tears dried. Obviously he was contemplating shitting himself daily.

'We can get two slices of fruit cake with it,' I said, eyeing the threepence. 'I'll go in for it,' I continued, 'you can't go into the shop like that.'

'Fuck off!' he shouted, his voice rising an octave.

'Little apples will grow again,' I said, smarting. I'd heard many big fellows say that recently. It was the 'in' thing, the classic saying of the period. I looked at his face for effect, but he started bawling again. Then he broke into a trot. I suppose he worried about what his Ma would say, having to wash his trousers. Few kids had a change of clothes then. Everyone was in the same boat, you didn't feel strange or put out. What you never had you never missed.

After the convent, something strange happened which was never fully explained to me nor understood by me. I should, of course, have graduated from the convent to a Catholic primary school. Through some error, possibly on my parents' side, my name didn't get entered in the new school at Crumlin. The school itself was bursting at the seams with millions of screaming kids who had sprung from the new estate. Having no place to go, my Ma took the unprecedented step of enrolling me in a Protestant school, which was, in fact, an orphanage. The front part was allocated for the education of Protestant children who lived in the vicinity. The building was situated in a place known as The Combe, famous in one of Dublin's best known songs, *Biddy Mulligan, the Pride of the Comb* (Boom, boom). The Combe itself was right in the heart of tenement land and only minutes from St Patrick's Cathedral, beloved of Dean Swift, the author of *Gulliver's Travels*.

The education system was far fairer than the Catholic system; at least it was in those cold and hungry days. All the children were taught in one large classroom, set off in sections by one very capable teacher whose name I have long forgotten. She was grey haired with glasses and she could spot a bright kid when she saw one. At the end of the day she would play the organ briefly,

her favourite melody being *The Road to the Isles*: Scotland must
have lurked somewhere in her background. This school was
sheer heaven compared to its Catholic counterparts. Always
without fail, five mornings a week there was a large tray of bread
and dripping laid out beside a steaming urn of sweet cocoa. One
sat and ate one's fill before starting lessons, even if one were
late. This was a great luxury because I was always hungry. The
orphanage at the rear of the building was our benefactor and the
children who would come and clear away the mugs and trays
fascinated me: it frightened me to think they wouldn't be going
home at three-thirty. I would cringe at the very thought of having
to remain in the same building 'til the age of sixteen, or was it
eighteen? Their cleanliness impressed me, they looked so well
scrubbed. But their cries haunted me, cries that reached our ears
when they were being chastised. Never a day went by without a
screech or yelp coming from the rear. The playing area was small
and securely partitioned off. 'No fraternisation' was the order of
the day. They, without exception, obeyed. Ogling each other was
a different matter. The boys and the girls in their black institu-
tional clothing and the urchins, such as we, dirty and bedraggled,
would gaze through the wire fence like one species of animal
surveying, with suspicion, the other. When school finished those
of us who lived any distance from the premises were given a
penny bus ticket. I, who lived about a mile or so away, qualified
for this free travel facility.

My ability to learn quickly didn't go unnoticed under the
watchful eye of our worthy teacher. The system was simple and
straightforward. If, say, after four months or thereabouts, you
were bright and leaving the other kids behind, you moved up a
standard, just like that — no waiting for a full term to elapse —
thus giving 'dickheads' a chance to catch up. Parties were given
once a month. Tray upon tray of mouth watering cakes, fizzy
lemonade by the gallon. Picture books and all sorts of little
presents to go with our paper hats made these the happiest days
of my entire school years. Whether they knew I was a Catholic or
not I'll never know, at the time it didn't cross my mind to worry
about it. The teacher probably knew. If she did, then she cer-

tainly kept my secret; for secret it remained. To her I was just another hungry kid, with an aptitude for learning — and learn I did. I skipped with selfish delight from second to fourth standard in one term. I was ten years old. The year was 1944. The War had swung in favour of the Allies.

It hadn't made much difference to us in Ireland. Bread was black; tea, sugar, butter, soap and clothes were rationed. Our family had not yet reached full strength. My Ma had more than enough of ration coupons, but you also needed money and that was sadly lacking. My mother supplemented her income by selling the surplus coupons — especially the clothes coupons. The little extra money she accrued went on other necessities, mostly food. The War though didn't miss us completely. In Dublin one horrible night a bomb was dropped a half a mile from our modest home. There was a lot of talk about the plane being British. I remember being awakened when the house shook violently. My father ushered us all out of bed and under the stairs. (This was supposed to be the safest part of the house.) The neighbours had run out of their homes and were talking nervously over the railings to each other, while we cowered in what, in fact, was the coal cellar. (That is, when there was coal.) Rumours were rife and arguments raged.

'It was British I tell you.'

'It was Gerry. Jaysus, didn't I see it?'

When it was confirmed that one of the buildings damaged was a Synagogue, people began to accept the German theory. Then somebody claimed that a fireman who was at the scene, and was related to his sister-in-law's uncle, had seen large stocks of tea and sugar hidden away in the Synagogue. 'Hitler knows what he's doing,' someone said.

The only other incident, far more serious, was when a land mine was dropped on the North Strand area of Dublin. Many people lost their lives in this incident and I remember vividly the damage which covered a wide area. My father brought me to the site the next day and held me aloft on his shoulders, above the heads of the crowds who had gathered to survey the horrific scene.

My schooling at the Protestant establishment was fast coming to an end because, unknown to me, things were happening behind closed doors. Discussions were in progress and the subject in question was 'yours truly'. Comings and goings from our hall door had sinister implications for my future education; an education which turned out to be a nightmare. On several occasions, a priest had called — once when I happened to be in. I was quickly ushered out of the house. I wondered at the time what it was all about, but my childish mind soon expelled any fears or doubts I might have had that it was to do with me and my daily feast of Protestant bread and dripping.

The school holidays were in full swing and I was out with many others scrumping apples or 'boxing the fox', as it was known locally. A nice bit of fresh fruit was always fitting and to have a dozen or so stuffed down the front of your jersey was the norm. I was still swallowing the iron medicine and having stone bruises lanced. It was a remarkably happy patch. Alas, not so for my mother, for the ugly head of religious wrath had loomed. Word had filtered back to the priest regarding my happy Protestant education. Pressure was being applied to my parents; it was a pagan attitude and it would have to stop. A place would be found immediately for me after the school holidays at The Christian Brothers, so my days were numbered. My Ma broke the news to me matter-of-factly.

'You won't be going back to the Coombe,' she said.

'Where am I going?' I asked, suspiciously.

'Crumlin,' she said, eyeing me.

'I'm not going to that shagging school,' I replied with an air of determination.

In an instant she had me by the hair and swung me round to meet her right hand. She slapped hard against my face.

'You'll do as you're bloody well told.'

The blow hurt and my eyes watered. I was pushed roughly into a corner.

'And there you'll stay, you little bowzie. You'll not get outside this door tonight.'

I slumped to the floor in anger. And in shock.

# Chapter 3

The school holidays ended for me with a heavy heart. I looked forward to the new term at the Catholic primary with foreboding and fear, not to mention sadness at the sudden loss of my daily bread and dripping, which was most revered and needed. Other children living in my neighbourhood had enlightened me. It seemed that some of the Christian Brothers who did the teaching were a force to be reckoned with. They wielded eighteen inch by two inch by half inch leather straps, which some used with sadistic pleasure. 'Hold out your hand', was the phrase which spelt terror to the would-be receivers. In all fairness, it has to be said that the pupils left a lot to be desired, a wild, hungry mob we were and certainly in need of control.

The morning dawned — or 'D-Day', call it what you will — when I had to enter the horror camp. I waited with mounting trepidation for my Ma to return from the weekly ritual of pawning my Da's suit. This morning, in particular, I was extra clean; my ears had been inspected with thoroughness.

My Ma held my hand firmly in hers as if she expected me to make a run for it, and believe it or not, the thought had crossed my mind. We approached the Catechism factory, in the company of hoards of yelling, screaming kids — fighting, biting, yelling, throwing stones — all generally adding to my terror. My history with the Protestant school had preceded me. I was somewhat of a celebrity, at least for a day. I was ushered into second standard: an instant demoting.

'He was higher than that,' my Ma offered vaguely.

'Yes,' intoned the Head, 'but what about the Catechism? And his Confirmation?'

I squirmed inwardly. My Ma agreed all too readily, she wanted rid of me and that was that. By the time the formalities were over the classroom was full. Thirty-six pairs of eyes watched me intently. I was shown my seat, amid speculative chatter. The teacher cracked down his leather strap on the desk and silence descended on the classroom in an instant. We were then motioned to stand for prayers. The indoctrination had begun. After prayers the Catechism.

The Ten Commandments were to be learned off by heart. First, I am the Lord thy God, etc. etc.: I was up to my arse in sin and prayer. Most of the morning was spent on that sort of crap. Several of the kids were told to hold their hands out. My mouth was dry with fear, lest I'd be asked to answer one of the horrible ten. We moved to another lesson, namely, Irish. This undoubtedly difficult language was beaten into us with the aid of the ever present leather strap. Bits of it had to be learned quickly as soon as it became apparent that if you wanted to visit the loo you had to ask permission in Irish — this resulted in many accidents! By lunchtime I had learned the loo bit off by heart, a relief in more ways that one. It sounded something like this: 'Wil cada dum gud a mot, mot shay the hulla.'

I emerged into the sunlight at twelve-thirty for a one hour break, bewildered, fed-up and hungry. I became friends with another lad who shared my desk and we ambled around the playground together. I voiced my bitterness to this lad whom I will call Joe. We became firm friends. He was overawed at my fourth standard form, and in the following months I did his homework as we walked home each evening. It was an easy, pathetic function to perform given my slightly higher standard of education. In return Joe lent a sympathetic ear to my constant invective regarding my plight. 'Why don't you mitch?' he said with finality.

'Mitch' was also known as 'Going on the prowl'. It was never referred to as playing truant. That was food for thought for it had never entered my mind at the previous school. Here I was being castigated and I had to climb the ladder of standards over again — all because I didn't know the Catechism. The afternoon session began again with the inevitable prayers, followed by reading, writing and arithmetic, all far too childish for me. Was I an old man at ten? My attention, or lack of it, soon landed me in trouble. I began to day-dream, my mind drifting back to the Coombe and the sadly missed bread and dripping. Suddenly my name was being called 'Purdy! Purdy!' (this time louder). That's me, I thought, jumping and becoming aware of the teacher's attention, aided by an elbow in the ribs from Joe.

'You are with us Purdy?'

'Yes sir,' I lied, feeling flustered.

'What did I say to the class then?' he asked. I clawed desperately for some clue, looking from side to side for a sign, anything to get me off the hook.

'Well,' he insisted, 'I'm waiting.'

Moments of eternity lapsed. 'You don't know, do you, Purdy?' Mockingly now.

'No sir,' I gulped.

'Come here,' he demanded with menace in his tone. I moved towards him slowly. I could feel the other kids' eyes boring into my back — almost hear their gloating: the 'pseudo-prod' was in for it.

'Why weren't you paying attention, Purdy?' The words fell from his lips, his eyes were alight with power, set in his pock-marked face. 'You weren't paying attention,'he repeated. 'Why?'

What could I say? I needed an answer and quick. 'Why, Purdy? Answer me.'

My heart sank. 'I was thinking sir,' I offered feebly.

'Thinking of what, Purdy?'

Oh Christ, bread and dripping, but I can't say that. 'Just thinking sir,' I said.

'So you can't remember what you were thinking about, Purdy?'

'No sir.' A titter ran through the class.

'Silence!' he snapped. 'Perhaps this will job your memory,' he said, producing the leather strap. 'Four of the best should make you pay more attention, Purdy. Well, shouldn't it?' he prompted.

One of the best would make me pay more attention, I thought, but I didn't say that, I simply nodded my head in agreement. He swished the leather strap through the air.

'Hold your hand out, keep it straight,' he said tersely. I watched the leather arch back above his shoulders. I closed my eyes. The sharp smacking sound of leather on skin rang out. I winced in pain. My arm buckled.

'Out straight!' he barked. I forced my hand out further. Another swish, crack and number two had landed. Three and four followed in rapid succession.

'Now we will pay more attention, won't we?' he leered. I mumbled a feeble 'Yes sir,' and put my hand under my armpit; not that it did any good, but I had seen other kids do it. I winced appreciably, lest I should get some more. I was ordered to return to my desk, which I did post-haste.

Four o'clock came at last. I'd never known such a long and terrifying day. Lessons came to an end with more prayers. I was beginning to feel like a monk! Suddenly the classroom door opened and in walked a man with a large tray of currant buns, one each. What joy, and to wash it down came a small, half pint bottle of milk. The coldness of the bottle soothed my still smarting hand. I gulped mine down. I was ravenous and it tasted delicious. The world was not a bad place after all.

Walking home later with Joe, I remarked in passing conversation that the bun and milk would have been more beneficial had it been issued at lunchtime. He looked at me as if I was a creature from another planet.

'Are you Jaysus joking?' he said. 'There would be no bugger at school in the afternoon if they did that.'

On reflection, Joe was right, because that bun and milk was probably the first bite some of the kids had had to eat that day. I was lucky, I'd eaten fried bread that morning.

School dragged on towards the Christmas break. I came to terms with the Catechism — I had to, it was less painful than the leather strap. Of course, the following year I had to make my Holy Confirmation. To be confirmed would make me a true and no-turning-back Catholic. Well, that was all in the future, which, to my young eyes, was formidable.

# Chapter 4

The Christmas I remember well was the first year that Santa Claus forgot us — no toys. It must have been very painful for my parents, too, being unable to afford presents for us all. My father had, in his own way, prepared us for the eventual disappointment.

'Bad boys and girls,' he intoned gravely, 'were left a bag of cinders.'

However, we still held hopes that we were good and worthy of gifts and had left notes under our pillows reflecting our wishes.

In the early hours of Christmas morning, we crept downstairs, Indian fashion, to see if Santa Claus had remembered. Apparently he hadn't, and my tearful disappointment was evident as we searched the parlour and kitchen. There were several boxes of cinders lying about and nothing else. I returned to bed, crestfallen, but was soon asleep again. I awoke later to a house filled with rejection. However, my Da did salvage something from the acute state of poverty in which we all found ourselves. There were boxes of Honeybee sweets and toffee as well as the boxes of cinders. My Da put on a brave face as he doled out the sweets saying, 'I told you if you weren't good you would get these,' smiling, all the while smiling.

Although we tucked into the toffees with gusto, we still had to emerge from the house later that morning to be confronted by hordes of other children dressed in cowboy suits and sporting six-shooters. Tram conductors suits were also in evidence, not to mention war parties of would-be Indians.

'What did *you* get?' was asked with a smirk from kids who knew damn well you got nothing. 'Cinders, I bet you got cinders. Holy Jaysus, cinders! Jaysus, Michael, did you hear that? He got cinders. Holy Jaysus it's gas. Your old man must be a mean old louser.'

And so the taunts continued. Later in the morning, things would brighten up. All one's relatives, or most of them anyway, would arrive for the annual gathering of the clan and, if nothing else was in the house, they could always count on a quota of 'gargle'. Four or five dozen bottles of Guinness plus a bottle of Jameson's whisky, accompanied by a bottle of port, were first on the priority list. These items were a must for every household, and they took precedence over all necessities.

When the other kids had tired of raking us, they got on with their games of cowboys and Indians. We, in our turn, kept watch on our uncles. They arrived Christmas morning and three pennies from each was the norm. My Ma always tried in vain to shoo us off, but we wouldn't be denied. Of course, our uncles knew we expected it and gave it accordingly, although they were as poor, or poorer, than ourselves. Before we got our three pennies we were always appraised: 'Jaysus, he's getting very big. He'll be a giant, Etta.' (Etta being my Ma's name).

'The image of his father. His mother's eyes though, God bless him. I hear he's a great singer.'

'Is that right?' another would say. 'Jaysus, let's hear him. The best of order now for Jim. Ah, Jaysus, you're not shy are you?'

''Course he isn't. Give the kid a chance. *A Nation Once Again* — give us that one.'

'Give him a sup of stout. He's a fine looking lad, Etta. Is he still taking that iron medicine? Doing him good too. Jaysus, he's grown. I think I'll have a drop of that iron medicine myself. His eyes are as blue as Dublin Bay. Who does he take after?'

'Ah, give us a song for Jaysus sake.'

And so it went on 'till they moved to another member of the family. When the bottles were cleared, and the glasses washed, the table was set for dinner. The table was made of pitch pine, years earlier, by my father. No doubt the timber came from The Guinness's Brewery. The tablecloth came out for his weekly airing every Christmas and Holy Day of Obligation, inclusive. Christmas dinner was always a full dinner in the true sense of the word. Turkey, ham and plum pudding, roast potatoes and mash, a cut of Christmas cake followed and a feeling of well-being ensued. Full bellies are better than toys but both together are the most preferable. Dinner over, we would be chased back out onto the streets to play and be taunted again. Tea time would see us creeping back in, not for our usual three cuts, but afternoon tea, biscuits and cake. How I longed for the whole box full of biscuits.

By St Stephen's Day, the disappointment of Christmas Day was almost forgotten. A feeling of hunger persisted, a longing for more cake and pudding. The inevitable hatred for school increased as the day approached for our return. The mornings were cold in January, thick with frost and possible snow. School at least was warm, the pipes were always hot and it was wise to warm your hands on them before entering the classroom, especially if you were late. To be late meant standing just inside the door of the classroom waiting to collect your four of the best.

'You're ten minutes late,' pockface would say menacingly. 'Why?'

'I was waiting for my Ma to come back from the pawn shop, sir.'

'Why?'

'To get my breakfast sir.'

'Couldn't you get your own breakfast?'

'There was no bread sir.'

'Hold your hand out.'

Swish, crack, pain. Your cold hands tingling from the frost, your feet bare and hurting too, as the warm air of the school brought the circulation back. The tears never far away, but proud and defiant, not wanting to cry in front of the other kids. The punishment over, your hand again under your armpit to squeeze out the pain; opening your Catechism with the left hand, and Joe whispering from the side of his mouth, 'Did it hurt?', and the joker directly behind you pinging your ear with his ruler.

One afternoon, the infernal morning Catechism lesson over and forgotten, a subtraction sum was written on the board. I'd already written the answer down on my copybook, positioning it

24

so that Joe could jot down the same answer. The teacher was always on the lookout for copycats. Fortunately Joe had a cast in his eye and it was difficult to pin-point the direction of his gaze. My attention was focussed on the kid's head directly in front of me. I'd seen a movement, and on closer inspection it became apparent that his hair was alive with lice — literally crawling with them. My eyes became transfixed; mesmerised if you like. It was not a sight that was new to me or, for that matter, to any working family in Dublin. We all had our quota of lice in our time. Indeed, our own household had crawled with the vermin, like any other house. That is to say, until the Free State Government took long overdue action and issued free boxes of insecticide, commonly known as DDT powder. It was marvellous and white and had wondrous qualities. I distinctly remember my mother spraying it in every conceivable corner of the house, particular attention being paid to the beds. DDT could still be had for free, so why was this kid's head in front of me practically walking? One did occasionally see a brown hopper, or flea, but a head full of lice was a glimpse from the past.

We, in those days, were plagued with all the fevers, diphtheria, scarlet fever, rheumatic fever, meningitis, rheumatics which invariably damaged the heart valves. My eldest sister, Margaret, contracted the latter and died of heart disease at the age of fifty. TB, or tuberculosis, was also rampant, and deadly. It was much feared. A cough and a spit, red with blood, fired one's imagination alarmingly and the Rosary beads would be shuffled incessantly through nervous fingers, imploring the Blessed Virgin, praying that one's fears were unfounded.

The fever hospital in those days was situated in Cork Street, between our home in Crumlin and my old school at The Coombe. It lay in fairly spacious grounds, right next-door to Donnelly's factory, famous for its sausage and pudding. Hundreds of pigs were slaughtered on the premises weekly, and the squeals from these unfortunate animals, who were dipped into scalding vats of water, couldn't have done much to lower the temperatures of the other unfortunates lying in their hospital beds.

The fever hospital devised a unique system of communication with the parents of the stricken children. Because poverty was rife and widespread some parents and relatives could not get to the hospital to see their loved ones: they couldn't afford the train or bus fare. Cork Street Fever Hospital serviced other counties besides Dublin. On admission each patient was allocated a number and this was communicated to the next of kin. The evening national daily newspapers did the rest. A large column was set aside for the patients, under the headings 'Serious', 'Satisfactory', 'Improving', 'Stable', etc., etc. You simply checked the number to know how your child was progressing. This hospital is now an old people's home and the modern fever hospital is situated in the South Dublin suburb of Clonskea. Through modern medicine, inoculations and vaccinations, the fevers, various as they were, have now been eradicated.

I was still engrossed with the lice. Gone from my world were 'sums' — adding, subtraction and Catechism. It was Joe's elbow again which jolted me back to reality. The un-Christian Brother was calling my name.

'Purdy, you're not paying attention.' The words were cold and impatient. 'Stand up when I'm speaking to you.'

I stood to my feet dejectedly. The inevitable 'Why?' boomed out. I finally blurted out the reason, pointing an offending finger at the other boy's head. The teacher walked down the row of desks, pausing at the one housing 'lice-head'. He didn't have to bend or stop for a close inspection. I noticed his nostrils wrinkle in distaste but he said nothing. Turning, he walked back to his desk slowly and purposefully. Fitting himself in his chair he opened a ledger which harboured our names and addresses. Reaching for a pen and paper, he began to write. Some minutes elapsed before he pressed blotting paper over the page, indicating that he had finished. Sealing it in an envelope he got to his feet and looked down upon the row of silent faces.

'Purdy!' he snapped.

'Yes sir,' I quickly replied.

'Take him home,' he said, naming 'lice-head', 'and see that his mother gets this. You might as well take your school bag too.

Don't bother coming back 'til morning.'

I went to my desk, hurriedly stuffing my few books into my school bag.

'Lucky swine,' Joe whispered. It wasn't yet two-thirty.

'What about my bun and milk?' I whispered back.

'See the caretaker,' Joe prompted. 'He dishes them out.'

I finally found the caretaker on the next floor. He'd already commenced to lay the trays of buns and milk outside the class-rooms. At first he wasn't very sympathetic, but relented when he saw the hungry look on our faces. Feeling fuller and happier now, I walked home with lice-head, clutching the letter in my hand.

'Bet this note is to tell your mother to get DDT,' I said knowingly.

Up 'til now this kid had shown very little concern for his pre-dicament, and was just as anxious not to miss out on his bun and milk as I was. Dragging his feet, bare like mine, along the ground he confessed opening, 'My Ma can't read,'

'What about your Da?' I asked unbelievingly.

'He's over in England,' he replied.

'Jaysus, there must be someone else at home who can read it?' I moaned.

'Oh, the woman next door will do it, she always reads me Da's letters when he sends me Ma her money from England.'

'Have you no brothers and sisters?' I countered.

''Course I have,' he replied, 'but they're all younger than me.'

'When is your Da coming home?'

'I don't know.'

'Did he not come home for Christmas?'

'No.'

'Why not?'

'I don't know.'

'Jaysus!' I said as we reached his house, which was exactly like ours. 'Here, give this to your Ma. Will she be in?, I said, waving the letter.

'I don't know.'

'Well, don't forget, I don't want to get the leather tomorrow.'

27

# Chapter 5

The winter marched on and gave way to spring. The Catechism lessons gained a new and painful prominence as the class prepared for Holy Confirmation. We were due to be confirmed in the month of May. The leather strap took its toll on our hands and we made steady progress at the expense of all other subjects. Confirmation was a simple enough process in itself, but not when it caused untold anxiety among the parents of the children who were to be confirmed. Appearances had to be maintained, each boy had to have a suit, shirt and, lo and behold, shoes! The money for these costly articles had to come from somewhere. The local women used to band together to form a money club, the number was usually twenty, those whose husbands had steady jobs. The selected twenty would gather at one of the homes and the numbers one to twenty would be deposited solemnly into a receptacle; the names would be duly dropped into a hat or such like. The draw would then take place amid gasps and groans — the latter if you were in the last ten. The first one out of the hat had twenty pounds to spend that first week, which was, of course, a fortune. These were the days long before the 'tally man' arrived on the scene. The twenty pounds was used to clear all debts such as rent arrears. A similar system was used by girls between the ages of sixteen and ninety. A bunch of them would converge on a local chemist shop and open a club credit account, invariably to the tune of ten shillings, repayable at two shillings a week, or sometimes less. This enabled them to purchase their war paint, 'cosmetics'. During this time, with the War rapidly coming to a close, nylon stockings — or silk if you like — were strictly under the counter and had a black market value well beyond a working girl's reach. The chemist had a good substitute though, in the form of a lotion. Its colour was tan and it came in a bottle. This was spread on the legs with one's hands, well above the knees, almost to the elastic of the then fashionable knickers.

Confirmation day arrived. I remember it well. There I was, resplendent and rather self-conscious in my first new suit. The shoes squeaked and hurt. The only consolation was a day off school. My photograph, too, was taken in company with the whole class and to the best of my knowledge, it was my first photograph — cameras and films were for the rich. My Confirmation badge hung from a red ribbon which in turn was pinned to my lapel; a sign to all and sundry that I'd finally made it.

The chapel that day was hot and oppressive and crammed with hundreds of nervous kids. The organisers, the Christian Brothers, our teachers, had the good sense to put all the dumb-witted kids in the middle of the pews, and those with a spark of brightness by the edge nearest the aisle. The bigwig who was officiating at the ceremony was certainly one of the top jollies, there was talk of him being a bishop. I'm unable to recall or confirm the rank he held in the Catholic church, but I do know that the congregation was conscious of the fact that a person of importance was present. After the service, during which we were told we would be stronger Catholics, this man of prominence walked slowly down the aisle, closely followed by his entourage. He paused now and again to ask a question on the Catechism. My heart raced as he approached my perch. Joe was well tucked away in the middle and safe. I closed my eyes and pretended to pray. He would pass me for sure, I told myself reassuringly. A deluge of surpluses seemed to descend on me like a cloud of locusts. I felt like getting up and bolting for the door. Then it was there — the touch, the hand.

'And you my child?' I looked up into a smiling benevolent face; a face full of compassion. His very presence oozed it.

'Are you feeling strong in your faith?' he probed gently.

'Yes Father,' I heard my hollow reply.

'And your name my child?'

'James Purdy, Father.'

'James is a nice name. Jim to your friends I suppose?' he teased.

'Yes Father.'

'Would you mind if I called you Jim?'

'No Father.'

'Well, Jim, name me the fifth commandment.' My mind raced and I panicked slightly before the words came to me like a well rehearsed song — First, I am the Lord Thy God … and I quickly rejected the first four in my head. Fifth …

'Thou shalt not steal.' I blurted with relief.

'Good boy,' his eminence said, giving me an affectionate pat on the head. There were smiles all round from his followers and from me pure joy. I glanced along the pew at Joe, a satisfied smirk on my face.

'An easy one,' he mouthed in return.

When I was back home, Ma lost no time in sending me round to the neighbours' homes. This was another way in which they helped each other, for the neighbours played their part well and clucked like a gaggle of geese. 'What a nice boy you are.'

Not forgetting to tell your Ma how nice your suit was and, of course, giving you what they could afford. Two pence, three pence, six pence or a shilling, and so on. That's what it really was all about — everyone helping with the cash. One's grand-parents had to be visited plus uncles and aunts. By the end of the day my pockets were bulging and I was beginning to believe I was gorgeous and had eyes like my Aunt Rosy and was the spitting image of Uncle Tucker.

It was late that evening, somewhere in the region of ten o'clock when the axe fell and my dreams were shattered. Home now after visiting all I could squeeze in, in the time allocated, my pockets were emptied by my Ma. The money was counted and stacked on the table in little heaps. I'll never forget the amount if I live to be a thousand — three pounds twelve shillings and a penny — and silly me was still under the impression that it was all mine. I was given a shilling and my mother reaped the rest of the harvest., Needless to say, I protested long and loud, but on reflection that was rather selfish of me. Tears and threats followed my entreaties for the return of the money. An open-hander across the face shut me up and I retired upstairs feeling very sorry for myself. I didn't see my suit again. No doubt it found its way over the pawn shop counter never to be redeemed. The next day I was relieved to be back in my bare feet; blisters on my ankles were sure evidence that I'd worn shoes the previous day.

With Confirmation over and done with the pressure was off. You could wipe your tail with the Catechism book; it had served its purpose and was now joyfully defunct. Joe and I began to go on the prowl and miss school, on average two days a week. We stood the punishment from parents and Christian Brothers alike. Joe had only one parent, his father, his mother having expired when he was an infant.

Fridays still came around each week and this fact seemed to keep everyone going — it was the one bright spot in our bleak existence. The summer months were eagerly looked forward to. Hiking was the name of the game and our destination never varied — Pine Forest. And we did hike, no buses or bikes, it was Shank's mare each and every week, weather permitting. The distance covered from Crumlin was about ten miles. I was always exhausted when I arrived but the sweet smell of pine burning at the camp fires made the effort worthwhile. The mountain stream, which ran through the forest, was ice cold and crystal clear. One Sunday morning, while drinking deeply this delicious water, I spotted two trout swimming to and fro. Even in those far off days I harboured great feelings for scenery and seclusion.

Most of the big camp fires were surrounded by members of bicycle clubs; older boys and girls — courting age, if you like. They always had plenty of food and didn't hesitate to share it. Seemingly all of Dublin was not poor but certainly all of Crumlin was. We, in turn, collected sticks for the camp fires, and, after stuffing ourselves on the generous helpings of sandwiches which came our way, joined in the evening sing-song.

As the day came to a close the fires would be dampened down, billycans tucked away in haversacks and the riders had a nice easy free-wheel back to the city. The lights could be seen twinkling in the distance. For us it was our marching song home. Walking downhill on a full belly was not too bad either.

*... Four men went to mow, went to mow a meadow,*
*For men, three men, two men, one man and his dog*
*Went to mow a meadow.*
*Five men went to mow, went to mow a meadow,*
*Five men, four men, three men....*

The song was endless.

It was a bitter pill to swallow when rain intervened and the weekly hike to Pine Forest had to be cancelled. The weekend was a heaven away from the horror and poverty that seemed to haunt us just a few miles down the mountain.

Half way between Crumlin and Pine Forest was Rathfarnham village. Just before the village was a river, The Dodder. It was, at that time, unpolluted. One section of it, which was rather deep — six feet or so — was known as Mollie's Hole. How it derived its name or indeed, its origin, is mystifying but if it was named after a woman she must have been mighty big. Yup, that there Mollie's Hole sure covered a heap of ground. It was at this infamous place that I learned to swim. Most of us swam in the nude; underpants were never heard of and swimming trunks were a luxury beyond reach.

Whatever I knew of reading, writing and arithmetic, I most certainly knew absolutely nothing about sex — absolutely and completely ignorant of the subject. I asked my Da on several occasions where I had come from, only to be told laughingly I'd been found under a head of cabbage. This state of affairs existed 'til I was twelve years of age, in spite of my Ma's often portly appearance and disappearance every eighteen months or so, only to reappear, nice and slim, carrying a new born baby. How stupid could I be!

Well, to get back to Mollie's Hole, certain men used to congregate there. Dirty old men too, although as I have said, I was completely unaware and innocent as to why they were present — onlookers as far as I was concerned. I'd heard words like 'brownies' and I knew that wasn't a name for girl guides. One summer's day, while sunning myself with half a dozen other kids on the river bank after a lovely refreshing swim, Joe and I, like the other kids, lay naked, stretched out, soaking up nature's gift. Anyway, there wasn't a towel between us. We were approached by a man who said simply he'd lost his collar stud, adding for effect: 'There's half a crown in it for the finder. It's solid gold'.

On hearing the mention of a reward, my ears claimed attention and I hoisted myself to a sitting position, as indeed did the other kids present. The man, it seemed to me, was paying particular attention to our private parts, and if you'll excuse the politeness and ignorance, the word 'endowed' wasn't part of my limited vocabulary then. Also, I hadn't paid much attention to the fact that the other kids had bigger and larger cocks than mine. Actually, when the penny dropped in later years, I realised I wasn't well endowed, far from it in fact. But back to the stud.

'Where was yer man's stud?'

He pointed to a spot in the long grass. 'It's there somewhere,' his finger stabbed the air. We were soon on all fours, as naked as a winter's tree — crawling and feeling our way with delicate fingers, scouring the spot indicated. However, we weren't the only ones crawling about; yer man was too and his eyes were undoubtedly appraising our young and tender bottoms. The roundness of our buttocks was making his breathing irregular to say the least; short sharp gasps. Suddenly, Joe, who was crawling alongside me, was whispering urgently; the message was loud and clear. 'He's a brownie!'

'He's not is he?' I countered, unwilling to show my ignorance and unable to comprehend.

Then a mighty shout echoed through this otherwise perfect summer afternoon.

'He's a fucking brownie.'

Instantly, we were on our feet running and running, as if a banshee was snapping at our vulnerable balls. I was well to the fore, as our small group headed in full flight for The Dodder Bridge, and me still not knowing what a brownie was. We all seemed to stop at once, as if an unknown hand had drawn down a barrier. We were, in fact, fleeing in the opposite direction to our clothes, in my case, shirt and pants. We'd put a fair distance of ground between ourselves and the would-be sodomist who was still heading in our direction.

'Get stone', someone yelled, and we piled into the river which was shallow at this point. Gathering up a handful each from The Dodder bed we emerged to advance on yer man, who now faltered and turned to flee. On seeing this we let out a yell and a cheer and took off in hot pursuit. On reaching the spot where our small bundles of belongings were heaped, we desisted — honour had been satisfied; could the same be said for desire?

I boned Joe on the subject later, after we'd dressed.

'Jaysus, don't tell me you don't know what a brownie is?'

Me, who used to do Joe's homework, had to admit defeat. Joe soon coupled some missing links as we headed home. The three mile walk was replete with gaudy detail. Joe was well versed on the subject, a subject which was taboo at school (sex education was non-existent in those days). I learned later that Joe wasn't the expert on detail that he professed to be, but he did start me on the right road to revelation. I was to find out also that the females of Dublin were far more advanced in the ways of the world than their comparable male counterparts.

The summer wore on with Joe and I fending for ourselves. The days we went on the prowl were spent selling newspapers. We usually arranged to meet near the school before heading for the city centre, and begged for a penny here and a penny there, always managing to raise a bit of cash. There were two Dublin evening papers, *The Mail* and *The Herald*. The first edition of *The Mail*, now defunct, rolled off the press about two-thirty and was sold wholesale at three farthings a copy — the retail price was three halfpence. Joe and I would normally start off with four copies, which cost us three pence, and naturally we endeavoured to sell them as quickly as possible. By doing so we would have doubled our money, then we'd repeat the process. People sometimes gave us two pence, aye, and on the odd occasion threepence. By our efforts and fleet of foot we could, and often did, earn a couple of shillings by the end of the day. This money was spent nourishing our bodies. 'Fish 'n chips' was ten pence (called a 'one and one'); a bag of broken biscuits cost three pence; a single bag of chips was four pence. Although these were fulfilling days in terms of food, they were marred by the knowledge that a good hiding awaited you on returning home.

Going home was left 'til the last possible minute — certainly never before eleven o'clock. Crumlin Christian Brothers had a foolproof method for getting at the truth regarding absenteeism. They simply sent another pupil to your home address, the result being, if you were playing truant, your Ma was alerted. Sometimes we lay in wait for these kids and threatened them with physical violence if they didn't return to the teacher with a supposedly genuine excuse; but some of the kids were cagey and often arrived at your home via unexpected routes. Some, too, didn't hesitate to tell the teacher that they'd been accosted and threatened, so the punishment was twofold: your Ma that night and your hand out the following morning for the ever-present leather.

Whatever chance I had, poor Joe had none. My trips to the dispensary were authentic — the iron medicine was still needed, and the infernal stone bruises still re-occurred at frequent intervals. Joe's one parent status didn't help. There was also the school inspector who cycled around the area stopping stray kids. He would jot down your name and address — even if you made a false statement it was difficult to outwit him, in fact almost impossible, because he had access to the school attendance register. The homes of the persistent offenders would be visited for explanations. It was into the clutches of a school inspector that Joe fell.

Although my mother hammered the living daylights out of me, she never failed to give a valid excuse if the inspector happened to call. I was increasingly becoming aggressive and punishment wasn't taken lightly: a strong feeling of injustice and revenge persisted, following the chastisement.

Once, later that summer, Joe and I discussed the possibility of running away. We were, at that time, in the seaside suburb of Dalkey, on the South Dublin coast. As usual, we were absent from school. We were studying the flotilla of small boats riding at anchor inside the breakwater.

'Listen,' Joe insisted, 'in any one of those boats we could get to England.' Joe was rabbiting on like some reincarnated Magellen.

'Where is England?' says I, fearful now in case he persisted.

'Over there.' Joe pointed his finger, indicating the distant horizon.

'Jaysus, you must be joking,' I hedged. 'We'd never make it.'

'Ah, you're yellow.'

'I'm not, honest I'm not. Cross my heart.'

'You shagging are.'

'Okay then!' I yelled. 'We'll see who's yellow! Let's go!'

We moved towards the steps leading down to the water. To this day, I don't know what would have been the outcome of this inclination had not providence taken a hand in the shape of a burly policeman. A proper redneck and built like a haystack.

'What ye two up to?' His voice boomed across the harbour like cannon fire. We both stopped in our tracks, shocked now at the sudden appearance of this giant of a lawman. He was approximately a hundred yards away and closing the gap by the minute.

'Stay where ye are.' Another broadside from the cannon rang out.

'Run for it!' yelled Joe. We both took off, gathering speed with every stride.

'Stop I tell ye!' roared the cannon.

I stopped, suddenly realising we'd committed no crime. Joe kept up a mad gallop and his arse soon disappeared into the distance. The redneck closed in and nabbed me by the hair. A clout on the ear was due next and I winced in anticipation.

'You're all right,' the cannon barked. 'You stopped when ordered.'

Nevertheless, I felt myself being pushed along, propelled by the scruff of the neck. The policeman, or Garda, was breathing heavily from the exertion of his short sprint. We walked for five or ten minutes and I assumed we were on our way to the police station. Passing by a parade of shops he hauled me into a doorway concealed from the road.

'What are ye two up to?' he demanded.

'Nothing sir. We were only looking at the boats.'

'Ye were going down the steps were ye not?'

'We seen something floating in the water, sir.'

'What did ye see in the water? Tell me that.'

'A bottle sir.'

'A bottle was it? Why then were ye going to see what it was if ye knew it was a bottle?'

'We thought there might be something in it. A message maybe sir.'

'You're a lying little bugger, are you not? Ye two were going to steal something from the boats. Tell the truth now and you can be off home.'

'No sir. We weren't going to lift anything.'

The questioning continued for some minutes until my pal came to the rescue. The Garda obviously knew the area and must have known Joe would appear along this particular pitch sooner or later. This is precisely what Joe did. He waltzed by the shop, whistling, and grab, the long arm of the law shot out from the doorway and Joe was in the bag. Corporal punishment was dispensed on the spot. Joe's head reeled from a series of blows, delivered by the open hand of the Garda. When honour was satisfied, we were both pushed roughly against the doorway. I knew if he asked Joe the same questions we were sunk.

'Why aren't ye two at school?'

A feeling of apprehension gripped me. Joe spoke first.

'It's our half day,' he sobbed, tears now escaping from his eyes.

'And what school gives ye half a day pray?'

'The shilling a week school,' Joe continued sobbing.

'And where might that be?'

'Crumlin,' I offered and silently congratulated Joe for a little nifty thinking, because such a school did exist.

'You be quiet,' the Garda insisted, jabbing a podgy finger in my vulnerable direction. 'Why would a school give its pupils half day? Tell me that.'

'I don't know,' Joe persisted.

'Well, it's a new one on me,' the Garda said suspiciously.

'I'm telling the truth,' Joe said, adding, 'we get a half day every Wednesday.'

In an instant the Garda had us by the hair. 'This happens to be Thursday,' he hissed.

The blood drained from my face. Realising the Garda was right, I cursed Joe inwardly. The two of us were ignominiously pushed onto the pavement. A heavy kick up the posterior followed; it hurt too, but we were free and legging it.

Further up the road we stopped to get our breath. There was a long walk home ahead of us. England was, by now, thankfully forgotten. Joe ragged me for stopping for the redneck and I retaliated.

'We were only running away from our own guilty consciences.'

We tried begging a few pence for our tram fare, without success. We suppressed our hunger by lifting some potatoes from a stall — three big ones each. Bumming some matches, we got a fire going on a patch of waste ground. Waste paper and twigs were gathered into a reasonable heap. Once the fire took hold, in went the murphys with their jackets on. Potatoes cooked in this manner are really tasty, and above all they're filling.

We were now fending for ourselves daily. Gone were the three cuts and the soup kitchen — to hell with that crap. Dublin was full of nice things and we would have them by hook or by crook. We both now smoked, sometimes bumming fags or even picking up the odd dog end. The Synagogue was a favourite haunt for scavenging 'butts', as cigarette ends were known locally. Shops sold smokes in quantities of one. American cigarettes were plentiful at three halfpence each, brands like White Horse, Black Cat, Lucky Strike and Camel, but to obtain such luxuries you had to have cash.

The following week, after our escapade at Dalkey, I was raiding an orchard. Actually there was only one tree in the back garden of this particular house, but it happened to be a pear tree.

The pears were big if a little on the hard side. They were easy enough to sell to the hordes at a halfpenny each. The only drawback was the house itself, it was owned by a redneck. He lived alone, undoubtedly a consolation for would-be scrumpers. The wall wasn't very high and over it like a stag I'd go. A monkey would be envious to see me scamper up a tree. My normal quota was six pears, which I would stuff down my shirt. The process would be repeated when the six were sold. I regarded this tree as my very own. Joe was the back-up man, keeping a lookout. The occupant of the house was never to be seen, but a neighbour who lived two doors away took it on his own back to be sole guardian over this solitary pear tree. He never failed to give chase, but by the time his back door would open, I'd be over the wall and gone. This happened so often that I soon got used to it. Joe would always lurk in the vicinity 'til he was satisfied that my pursuer had returned indoors, then beckon me back to work. I would trot back the hundred yards or so which I'd put between myself and my antagonist. Then the inevitable happened — the back door slammed shut, but the would-be Sir Galahad remained outside, creeping to the end of his garden to stand motionless and out of view. I arrived back on the scene after Joe had signalled the all clear. In seconds, I was up the tree, but before I could pluck a single pear this idiot was crashing through his back gate. I was nabbed, caught red handed.

'It's not your shagging tree,' I heard myself say.

'And what right have you to steal from it?' he countered. He was a bespectacled chap in his thirties. I might have talked my way out of it but for another stroke of bad luck. Within minutes of my being caught, who should turn into the lane but the owner, the Garda, still in uniform just coming off duty. My heart disappeared downwards: he was built like the north face of the Matterhorn. If I'd been a little frightened earlier, I was now scared stiff.

'Pinching me pears are ye?' he roared, with the pitch of a force ten gale. 'Let's have you,' he grated, yanking me into orbit.

He threw me across his shoulder, fireman fashion, and stormed off towards the police station, a quarter of a mile up the road. A howling mob of kids brought up the rear, yelling for my blood. My tears were real and many by the time we reached the station. He planted me in front of the desk sergeant who spoke rapidly in Irish to his colleague, now standing directly behind me. A smile crossed his lips.

'Caught in the act,' he said, glaring at me. 'The punishment is death. You know that, don't you?' he declared.

'No sir,' I cried with greater urgency.

'Which would you prefer — hanging or shooting?' His voice rising to emphasise this rather startling statement. 'Well … I'm waiting,' he continued.

'I don't want either,' I managed to whimper.

'What! After stealing all those pears? Do you think we should let you go then?'

My head shook up and down indicating a decisive 'yes'.

'Good God! Do you hear that, John, he doesn't want to be hanged, and shooting is a nice clean death. But no, he doesn't want that either.'

I heard a distinct chuckle from behind me, followed by another rapid discourse in Irish.

'Very well, John. You're a kind man. Do you know what he said?' the sergeant queried.

'No sir,' I replied, tearfully.

'He is giving you a chance, you little blackguard. Now go, and I don't want to see your face in here again.'

I kept the tears rolling as I approached the door. I was quick to notice John was positioning himself to give me a parting kick in the pants. I tried to avoid his eyes and shuffled the first few steps before finally making a dash for the open door, but I was too slow, far too slow. I could feel the toe of his boot connect. I was airborne for half a dozen strides, my tail hurt painfully but I landed on my feet, still running. The howling mob of kids was still by the gate of the police station.

'What happened Purdy?'

'What did they do to you?'

I pushed and elbowed my way through with the help of Joe, who was tugging and pulling to clear a path. My tears ceased as

we raced towards Dolphin's Barn, a village on the canal cut —
just down the road from nearby Crumlin. The mob soon tired of
chasing us. Joe and I took refuge under the canal bridge. Fortunately Joe was holding the money which we had accrued by
the sale of the pears. Three lots of six all sold at a halfpenny —
the total cash in hand, nine pence. Making for the city centre, we
converted this cash into first editions of *The Evening Mail*. Soon
we were jogging at a steady pace through the pubs and betting
shops.

'*Mail*! Get your *Mail*! *Evening Mail* sir?'

Later that evening we shared our dough — one shilling and
eight pence each — which went on chips, smokes and the
pictures. My bottom was still sore, but both our bellies were full.


Back at school it was the usual crap. Joe was worried — he'd
had a summons for non-attendance. It was serious, because one-
parent kids didn't stand much of a chance in Dublin's juvenile
courts. Bad attendance at school was frowned on, to say the least.
The lousy part about the whole set-up was the end result, which
was inevitably Artane. This was a large, sprawling, industrial
school which was situated in a suburb of Dublin north of the city.
Kids were normally sent here 'til they reached the age of sixteen,
to be educated and learn a trade at the same time; the education
being left to the ever-present Christian Brothers. The trade took
the form of working in the self-sufficient market gardens, repair-
ing boots and shoes, or you might end up in the Artane Boys'
Band, where you would see the outside world again at functions
such as the All Ireland Hurling Final or other Gaelic gatherings.
Whatever else Artane did for Dublin's youngsters, it succeeded
overwhelmingly in one endowment — terror. The very name of
it sent shivers down one's spine. It was to such a place Joe was
sent. I couldn't believe it. My young mind was numb with shock.
My pal, my china, was put away. Joe was twelve years old then,
he had four years to serve.

By the age of fourteen he was dead. He had hanged himself.

# Chapter 6

It was years later before the other activities that went on in Artane were brought to my attention from a man who had spent six years in that God-forsaken hole.

I don't want to incriminate all Christian Brothers because, needless to say, good Christian Brothers did exist. However, there were some whose actions are unforgivable. In Artane there were large dormitories for large groups of boys. Each dormitory had a small cubicle set aside, just inside the dormitory door: a Christian Brother slept in the small room, undoubtedly to keep the children under surveillance (that was the theory). What at times happened was that the Christian Brother would have his fancy boy — some poor unfortunate youngster picked out of the bunch for his sole sexual pleasure.

These children would be given an apple or an orange for being a good boy, before being sent back to their bed. This sort of situation existed under the very noses of — indeed, was perpetrated by — those who opposed birth control and who religiously went to Mass and Holy Communion every day. Never should any bunch of kids be left solely in the hands of older celibate men, matrons and married couples perhaps, but never celibates.

What really drove Joe to top himself? I have never discovered the answer. We were not saints, nor sinners either, just victims of circumstances, and above all just youngsters.

Other pals and buddies came into my life such as Noel, Paddy, Michael, John and Charlie; all more or less lived in the same street. My schooling days were coming to an abrupt end. I was twelve, the War was over. On our road, two men had died fighting for His Majesty's Forces and several had received wounds. There was plenty of work across the water and a lot of big fellows disappeared in the general direction of England. Letters and much needed money were arriving home and stories of inflated wage packets were commonplace. Needless to say, these sort of tales were egging others to head out for the promised land. The amounts stated in these letters could be disregarded and treated as blarney; as for the work — yes, there was plenty of it over yonder for the taking. I had itchy feet, like most of the nomadic Irish, but to leave home at the age of twelve was out of the question.

The currant bun at school was now discontinued. In its place we were given a cheese sandwich, and on alternate days it was bread and jam. It was all welcome. One day I was ordered from my desk — it was an Irish lesson with which I had trouble, and try as I might I just couldn't grasp the vowels. It was like some horrible, monstrous unsolvable jigsaw. The hidings of leather had increased from four to six. The brother swished it in the air as he approached the corner where I cringed, in the expectancy of the harsh punishment.

'Six Purdy,' his voice said, betraying no emotion. 'Hold out,' he roared. 'Out with it Purdy, or you will get eight.'

I gulped and heard myself say, 'No.'

'Hold out your hand Purdy!' This time he hissed the words between thin lips. One could feel the tension in the classroom mounting.

'I'm waiting Purdy,' he said again. I kept my hands firmly behind my back and said nothing. There was no backing out now; I was fully and totally committed to disobey. I noticed the colour of his face change and a rage appear that hadn't been there before. I felt more scared now than I'd ever been. The seconds ticked by. I was beginning to wilt under the mounting anger of a grown man. He let the strap drop to the floor. By now I was weak with fear. I was jerked off my feet with terrific force and swung round towards the middle of the classroom. One of his legs went behind mine, then he pushed me bodily backwards.

With my balance gone, I was on the floor, spread-eagled, my arms pushed out and his knees keeping them pinned down. All this happened in an instant. He immediately began raining blows to my head with both fists. I struggled and strained, and after some minutes managed to free one of my arms. I made a grab for his nose, two fingers grasped it, pincer fashion. Then I twirled and twisted with all the venom and frustration that my young years had accumulated. His face became purple with distress. He'd stopped hitting me by now and was hastily endeavouring to loosen the vice-like grip I had on his hooter. When I did eventually release my hold he just sat back on his bottom and gurgled. Suddenly, blood gushed from his nose at an alarming rate. I scrambled clear, but not before I was liberally sprayed with my attacker's blood. He managed to struggle to his feet, reaching his desk for a handkerchief. He forced his head backwards in an effort to stem the flow of blood which by now seemed to be everywhere.

I stood back in the punishment corner, my eye felt puffed as did other abrasions and his blood over my only shirt wasn't going to please my Ma either. Eternity lapsed before the Brother stemmed the flow — his black cassock looked in a mess. Finally, he gathered some sort of composure and made for the classroom door, without as much as a word or a backward glance he was gone. Now it was the kids' turn!

'Purdy, he's gone for the head. He'll shagging kill you. You'll be murdered.'

'Why didn't you hold your hand out? Were you afraid?'

'Jaysus, wait 'til me Ma hears this.'

'Purdy, run for it. Don't just stand there for Jaysus sake. Go on, you shagging idiot.'

I didn't move. I stood there as if held by some centrifugal force. A good fifteen minutes lapsed before the door opened again — he was back. He'd obviously been over to his quarters to change his cassock. He looked clean and tidy. He walked over to where I was standing, a look of distaste on his face. I didn't know what to expect. He paused before me, looking down on what must have been a wretched, scared kid.

'Go home Purdy,' he mumbled softly. I thought I was hearing things.

'Purdy, go home,' he said again. I heard a door open. He was standing there, holding it by the handle.

'Go home Purdy,' he repeated, almost with resignation. 'And don't come back.'

The sense of relief I felt was overwhelming. I was out in the corridor running, lamming it as fast as my legs would carry me. The main door loomed ahead and beyond that the main gate., These I negotiated swiftly and turned in the general direction of home. A feeling of pure, joyous elation coursed through my body. 'Don't come back' — those words ran through my brain: pure magic. I rushed home, breathless but happy. My Ma was none too pleased as she rinsed out my shirt and put it to soak in cold water. She could see I'd been through the mill. She wheedled the truth out of me, bit by bit, with the ever-present threat of more punishment.

'You will have to go back to school,' she said finally.

'He doesn't want me back,' I protested.

'You're going back and that's that,' she said. 'First thing in the morning too,' she added for good measure. 'You're not running around the streets, causing mischief. I've worries enough as it is.'

'I'll get a job,' I pleaded.

'Where would you get a job at your age, I ask you?'

On and on it went. The next morning, true to form, my Ma took me back to school. She had waited 'til all the other kids had been whistled in from the playground. She held me firmly by the hand as we waited for prayers to finish. Finally she knocked. The door opened and there he was, my adversary. A lot of small talk ensued between my mother and the Christian Brother, then the same magic words.

'Sorry Mrs Purdy. He's wild. I've no control over him whatsoever.'

'Did you hear that?' my Ma said, looking down at me and giving me a stinging clip on the ear. I managed to squeeze a solitary tear, I had to make it look good. Inside I was feeling exultant.

'Sorry,' I heard the Brother's voice again as the door closed. This time it was closed for good.

I was never to set foot inside a classroom again, and so a period of my life ended. Looking back now I can say, with all honesty, that I haven't one happy memory of the time spent at Crumlin Christian Brothers School for Boys.

# Chapter 7

I was now a 'louser' — a name reserved for one who didn't go to school or to a job of work. My mother did her best, trying hard to coax me into entering another school, but I'd had enough. I was twelve years old, my top front teeth had decayed, they had never felt a toothbrush across their surface. I was sleeping on the floor along with two other brothers. The family had increased and beds were scarce.

My earning potential was drastically reduced too. Late one evening, when endeavouring to sell the last two copies of *The Evening Mail*, I was stopped by two burly men who turned out to be plain clothes policemen. The result was I was charged with selling newspapers without a permit or badge — what a brilliant piece of detective work!

While standing there, parting with my name and address, at least another dozen kids came running by, shouting, '*Herald* and *Mail*! Get your evening paper!'

I duly appeared before the magistrate, accompanied by my Ma, and was fined five shillings; a costly fine which she had to pay. To make matters worse, she hadn't realised until then that I was in the newspaper business. Another clouting was the result – no doubt with the five shillings in mind.

Those early days of being evicted from school were lonely ones. All the other children seemed to be toeing the line and the streets were pretty devoid of kids. Shuffling around the streets on your lonesome wasn't much fun — no one to scheme with. Robbing orchards was old-fashioned and childish.

The funerals in those days were horse drawn affairs, the cortege being made up mostly of walkers who trudged behind (poverty again), either to Glasnevin or Mount Jerome. The former, known as the dead centre of Dublin; the latter, Mount

Jerome, was near Crumlin, situated at a place called Harolds Cross, and many a funeral I attended there — especially if it was accompanied by a band, such as preceded a soldier's or policeman's hearse.

A little further down the road was an establishment called The Hospice Of The Dying. (Who on earth chose such names?) We youngsters frequently visited the premises, although I never fancied going in there alone. 'The Dead House', as it was called, was an outbuilding where the recently departed were laid out on marble slabs, their stiff white heads resting on clean white pillows. This place was, and is, run by nuns, and oddly enough the slabs were always occupied; the death rate must have been very high indeed. I mention this because I got the fright of my life one sunny afternoon. The Dead House was open to the public seven days a week, where relatives and friends could view their beloved ones on their demise. A small altar was in evidence, there were candles which one could light and place on the altar, where a prayer could be offered for the repose of the unfortunate soul. The ever-present donation box was in a handy position. It was deemed the thing to do to offer a few pence for the candles.

Anyway, to get back to the scare I experienced: an old and very dead woman lay on one of the slabs, 'gone as sure as the Dodo'. No different to any of the others present, except for her feet, which protruded from beneath a shroud. Nothing unusual in that either, for the exposed parts of all corpses were heads, hands and feet; the hands always crossed, as if in prayer. This old woman's remains differed slightly. Her big toes were tied together with a red ribbon, the actual knot being a bow. We gathered around this particular corpse to discuss the ifs and wherfores, because we hadn't seen the like of it before. There were two other kids present besides myself, and I won't say who, except it wasn't me, who slipped the knot. Suddenly the two legs sprang outward. The complete unexpectancy of it paralysed the three of us with fear, momentarily, of course, and I can assure you it was only momentarily. I heard a cry of 'Jaysus!' from one of my 'oppos and it came from behind me, for I wasn't last. I could hear the pitter patter of two sets of bare feet close on my tail. The distance through the tree lined grounds must have been two hundred yards. I would think we set some sort of record that day. We collapsed against the wall outside the main gate, our mouths open and gulping fresh air, as if it had just come off ration. Some minutes passed. We still sat there waiting on our heart beats to return to normal. Two women walked by with shopping bags and one remarked, 'Deborah, those youngsters look very pale. You'd think they'd seen a ghost.'

I never entered the hospice of the dying again and hope I never will. We walked home along the canal in silence, pausing now and then to skim a slate across the water. The sight haunted me for days and I didn't know the answer then and wouldn't dare ask my Ma or Da. After all, who wanted a clip on the ear?

Shortly after that incident my circumstances were to change slightly for the better. A greyhound trainer of some repute, whose kennels at times housed up to thirty-six dogs, gave me a part-time job, exercising the hounds. His name was Jack Davis. I would say he was one of the greatest authorities on greyhounds Ireland had, or ever will, produce.

Four dogs at a time, two in each hand, were walked to a certain point along the canal, then back to the kennels for four more. In their absence, the straw would be changed and the kennels disinfected. A strong smell of Jeyes Fluid was always in the air. Distemper and Hardpad had yet to be conquered.

The greyhounds in Ireland are trained off the track, as opposed to their British counterparts who are mostly trained at the track where they race. The distance covered on the daily walk for each group of dogs was three miles. Later in the evening they would be taken for a short stroll around a nearby field to empty their bowels and bladders. Jack and his brother Bert would be at the evening meeting. The two dog tracks were Shelbourne Park (not far from my place of birth) and Harolds Cross, almost directly opposite Mount Jerome cemetery. Every dog had to be exercised. A sure sign that he hadn't been out of his kennel would be a telltale heap of shit lying on the floor of the kennel the next morning. This would bring a good telling off from Jack and a clip around the ear for good measure. During this period I could have bettered by Da's financial circumstances with a little inside information.

Men with ferrets and nets would call at the kennels occasionally. These were the trappers who made their living rabbiting; blocking off the various exits from the burrows with their nets and letting the ferrets do the rest. Live hares were in great demand, fetching a price of fifteen shillings, whereas live rabbits carried a tax of only five shillings. The reason was simply that the unfortunate hare died screaming a high pitched screech, like a child in great pain; the rabbit dies a silent death — whether through fright or nature, I don't really know. All the live rabbits I fed to the cruel jaws of greyhounds expired without uttering a sound. The method by which these executions were implemented was sadistic but necessary for the well-being of the greyhounds concerned. A hind leg of the chosen hare or rabbit would be broken and attached to a long rope, anything up to one hundred yards of rope would be used — the hare or rabbit would reach the end of the rope and double back, this process would be repeated until the greyhound closed in for the kill. The rope was mainly to avoid injury to the dog and it guaranteed a certain kill. A dog trying that evening at the track would be 'tuned-up' by this method in the afternoon.

My Da had to pass the kennels on his way home from the brewery. I had quickly realised that the live kill was a tip in itself, so naturally I began to watch out for him, armed with the red hot information. My Da always had the evening paper stuck out in front of him, as he walked he was reading. I remember vividly rushing towards him one evening, shortly after giving a certain dog a hare.

'Da,' I whispered breathlessly, 'I just gave so and so a live hare.'

He lowered his paper slowly and deliberately, looked me straight in the eye and said simply, 'I'm not interested in dogs.' He then raised his paper to his nose and walked on towards home.

I felt both frustrated and annoyed as I trudged back to the kennels. I tried the same tactics time and again but to no avail. He just wouldn't back a dog. To his dying day it was horses only.

# Chapter 8

These were well fed days for me. The iron medicine and stone bruises were behind. Boots were on my feet, thanks mostly to the trainer and his owners. To use an old Irish phrase — they were terribly decent men.

I did other jobs besides exercise the hounds. Each day I went to the bakers and bought all the stale brown bread left over from the previous day; usually enough to fill a sack. Then down to O'Keefe the knackers for a stone of horse meat. This would be boiled in a huge caldron with mixed vegetables. The brown bread would be mashed through it to thicken it up. I always had my whack before the dogs — delicious and highly recommended.

On top of that, most evenings I would go to a field adjacent to the kennels where a small herd of cows grazed peacefully. Armed with a bucket, I would grab the nearest one and milk it; the squirts of milk making tinny noises on the bottom of the bucket. I would then spike my thirst on the luke warm liquid.

Another money earner those days was minding bikes. Simply choose a pub, a busy one preferably, and as the customer dismounted rush to him and shout, 'Mind your bike sir?'

I say 'rush' because there was always competition. Other kids had the same idea. Thursdays, Fridays and Saturdays were the best nights for business. After a couple of weeks you were familiar to the customers and in that way would build up a clientele. The average fee was two pence, and you often had to stand vigil 'til closing time for your money. Sometimes a client would appear the worse for wear and deny ever having given you permission to mind his bicycle, and possibly aim a blow at your head for good measure. In instances such as this you made

51

yourself scarce.

Nowadays, when I see a Lowry painting depicting his match-stick people wandering aimlessly in the foreground, I ponder why he didn't paint some of his subjects on bicycles. Wasn't Lancashire working class with lots of its inhabitants dependent on the bike? It was a common sight in Dublin to see cyclists riding six abreast during rush hour, buses and bikes, but very few cars, the latter only for the privileged.

Circumstances at home eased somewhat with the first four born now working. They weren't earning a great deal but it helped. In one way and another it brought problems. The full thirteen were living in a two-bedroomed house with the eldest now in their teens needing a little privacy. Also they were becoming more aware of appearance — new dresses and suits were required, not just a clean shirt.

Job opportunities were few for boys with a poor background, and one usually began by riding a messenger bike. Young girls found themselves in some small clothing factory, sewing buttons or hems.

I could not ride a bike then, but managed to land my first real job pulling a handcart at ten shillings a week. It was a fairly large factory manufacturing ladies' clothes. One of my duties was tending the boiler. The manageress simply pointed to the gauge on the side of the boiler and warned: 'Don't let it go above the red mark.' Indicating of course, the pressure gauge.

So between stoking the boiler and loading large brown parcels on to the handcart, my regular working days began. Needless to say, I was thrilled when I landed the job and rushed home to tell me Ma. She was not too happy about it, saying I could get into trouble, referring, of course, to my age. However she consented with a sigh of resignation, maybe for no other reason than that it might keep me out of mischief.

I pulled the handcart over the cobbled streets of Dublin like a proud horse. I knew the city well and had no trouble with navigation. Friday loomed after what seemed a very long week. I just couldn't wait to get my hands on my first pay packet. At about three thirty on Friday afternoon the wages were brought round by the manageress on a tray. I received mine without much ado. It was not very fat. In fact, it contained a ten bob note.

I walked home not wanting to change the note for the bus ride. Feeling as proud as a peacock, I realised for the first time what Friday really meant to the average Dubliner. A sort of relaxed happy atmosphere existed. Smiling, grateful faces were to be seen. The wage packet had solved their immediate problems, worries could be put aside until Monday. It was that very afternoon I heard two girl machinists chant as they worked — *Come a day, go a day, God send Friday*. I handed my mother the pay packet with a surge of pride. She gave me a little hug and asked, 'Are you sure you're able for it?'

I reassured her of my desire and ability to hold the position. I was then given half a crown pocket money. I was now bringing money into the house, contributing to the pot, and justifiably felt I was one of the big fellows. After all, I was working, wasn't I? Who needed school kids for pals?

At this stage in my life I hadn't experienced any sexual desire and was devoid of pubic hair. It was still for passing water, despite poor Joe's earlier lesson. The clothing factory employed another lad — a biggish lump of a chap aged about seventeen. He was very handy for getting the heavy bales of cloth from the basement, where they were stored, to the cutting room upstairs. One day, while skiving on top of a heap of bales, he broached the taboo subject of sex. I pretended to know more than I did, while he in turn kept staring at the ceiling above our heads.

'Just think,' he muttered. 'All those mots sitting up there.' Indicating the ceiling. (Mot was the local jargon for girl.)

'All virgins,' he cracked, now warming to the subject. 'Have you ever done this?' he said, his voice sounding peculiar.

He took out his penis and commenced masturbating. Very soon he was in a little world of his own. I, for my part, didn't realise what he was doing, and sat there overawed as this spectacle unfolded before my eyes. (I wasn't to feel any sexual stimulation of the groin 'til I was almost fourteen.) When he climaxed he turned to allow the white sperm to spew out onto a bale of cloth. Returning his penis to its holster, he declared solemnly, 'That stuff,' indicating his sperm, 'cures foot and mouth disease.'

I'd often seen herds of cattle being driven through the streets on their way to be slaughtered, cattle that had blisters on their mouths, and I knew this to be foot and mouth disease., I looked at the pool of sperm again before finally replaying 'Shagging liar!'

It was something to do with sex, that much I'd ascertained, but what? I was unable to comprehend the deed committed and unwilling to display my ignorance. He repeated this act on several other occasions. Later in life I was able to put a tag on it. He was most definitely a flasher.

The job didn't last too long — about six weeks in fact. The end came abruptly and unexpectedly. I was out pulling the cart which was stacked with six large brown paper parcels, trudging wearily around the city to the various dropping points. No problems arose until the second last point of delivery. Entering the building, dropping the parcel, having the invoice signed, took only minutes. I re-emerged into the daylight to find the cart empty, the parcel gone — hooked. 'Lifted' was a term used then, but gone it was. My heart sank on seeing the empty cart. I looked quickly up and down the street. There were plenty of people in view but no sign of anyone lugging a large brown parcel. I panicked a little, realising I could be blamed, indeed, accused of taking it. 'Accomplice' and 'Accessory' were words I understood and feared.

I re-entered the shop which I'd just left and explained, with growing despair, my plight. The manageress seemed genuinely concerned about my predicament and actually 'phoned the firm on my behalf. I haltingly related my movements to the manageress stating all the deliveries I'd made — five in all. She quickly informed me that the missing parcel contained five hundred aprons, giving me explicit instructions to contact the first policeman or police station I encountered, whichever came first.

I was in a side street off a far busier thoroughfare called Dame Street. The nearest police station was in College Green. I had to negotiate Dame Street to get there and it was in this street, while pulling my cart despairingly, that I spotted a redneck. He stood on the edge of the kerb and appeared to me as if he'd had a good skinful.

To put the record straight, the term 'Redneck' was a word used to describe literally any person who was not a Dubliner. Up from the country 'culshies' — men of the soil who, while continuously tending their half acres or cutting and turfing their section of bog, would acquire a red neck from the sun, while bending their backs. To the 'redneck' a Dubliner was a 'Jackeen'. There was a friendly rivalry, in that nothing sinister lay behind the remarks. I drew abreast of the policeman and rested the cart.

'Excuse me sir,' I began.

He listened in silence, his eyes registering a little annoyance at my interruption. When I'd finished, he opened his mouth and uttered the most incredible words I'd ever heard.

'Nothing to do with me,' he declared, hooking his thumbs in his tunic.

'Are you on duty sir?' I offered, unable to comprehend this unexpected twist.

'Get down to the station,' he bellowed — his face reddening to match his neck.

I made a mental note of his number which was displayed on his tunic lapel. Then getting between the shafts again, I headed for College Green station. The first words the station sergeant (who incidentally was another redneck) spoke when I'd finished relating my tale of woe yet again were, 'There're plenty of police patrolling the streets. Surely you passed one on your way here?'

It was now almost an hour since the discovery of the theft and I immediately told him of my encounter with the other redneck.

'Ah, but did you get his number?' he asked triumphantly.

'I did,' I replied with equivalent relish.

His eyes widened at this declaration. He then began to jot down the details of the missing aprons. I thought afterwards if the thief or thieves got one shilling each for them it would amount to a colossal twenty-five pounds, a year's salary for me!

It was now only a matter of time before my first venture into employment came to an end. The missing aprons left a cloud over my head which wouldn't easily disperse. I had a guilty conscience — don't ask me to explain the feeling. It seemed I'd let the whole side down, and people were peering at me from around every corner. The manageress was very nice about it. The firm was fully insured. I didn't get a ticking off, although I really expected one. The rednecks didn't get yer man either and the wanker was still doing his daily dozen. He said he was sorry to see me go.

I bet he was too.

# Chapter 9

The next step in my working career was a bit of an uplift. I left the shafts of the cart to be elevated to the saddle — a bicycle saddle. There were jobs for messenger boys around the more fashionable suburbs like Terenure and Rathmines. Lots of these houses had maids living in, known to us as skivvies. At this stage in my life I'd never ridden a bike, simply because I'd never owned a bike. One of my elder brothers Brian, was already in the messenger service. I used to wait patiently for him to come home for lunch, take his bike and scud along the road with one foot. When I'd gathered enough speed I'd lift my other leg up. This method helped me to gain balance. It took a great deal of courage before I managed to throw my leg over the crossbar and many a fall was taken before the art was mastered. After a couple of weeks of this I felt proficient and decided to chance my arm on the coming Monday.

Messenger boys either gave their job away on Saturday or were dispensed with. Pay day was Saturday in this game and it was not until the last minute — which could be eleven at night — you picked up the pittance, commonly known as 'wages'.

I took myself to Rathmines, my eyes eagerly searching the shop windows for the telltale sign, usually a square piece of white paper with the magic words written in large black capitals, 'MESSENGER BOY WANTED. APPLY WITHIN'. That Monday Rathmines was devoid of vacancies and I decided to try Rathgar, making my way there via the tram route. I soon saw what I was looking for. It was a large shop and employed several messenger boys. The interview was brief and to the point — had I been in other employment?

'Yes.'

'How long for?'

'Six weeks.'

Could I produce a reference?

'No.'

'Sorry, we don't employ anyone without a reference.'

Back on the pavement I cursed out loud and headed for Terenure, my next stop. Each and every shop was scanned, all to no avail, before turning and heading for Crumlin, past the rubbish tip along Sundrive Road into Down Patrick Road, my place of residence.

It had taken me all morning and my legs ached. I sat on the step by our gate, not a farthing in my pocket. I'd looked in all those shops full of mouth-watering goods — things that had certainly never crossed our doorstep. Some people seemed to be well-off, well-dressed, well-fed, well-schooled, well-bred and well-housed. It was sinking in at last: we were the dregs, nothing, fucking cheap labour, ignorant too, and as common as a twenty-four hour day.

I entered the house for a drink of water. Putting my mouth under the running tap, I slurped and gulped the cold liquid down to keep the hunger at bay. It always seemed to be gnawing away, deep down in your guts. My teeth ached, the cold water having seeped into the exposed nerves of infected gums. There was no one else indoors, my Ma had been to the pawn shop and was now gone shopping with the youngsters who were not yet ready for school. When she returned I was sitting by the front gate again, my hands nursing my face. The pain was excruciating. My upper front teeth were just black stumps. Not a very pretty sight to look at. Being at an impressionable age, I was aware that other kids had nice white teeth. I was feeling rather low when my Ma appeared with the shopping. Seeing me sitting there was enough. However, she paused and said, 'No luck?' I shook my head.

'Does your teeth hurt?' she said in a sympathetic voice.

'They do,' I replied, pinching my gums endeavouring to get some relief.

'I am making a sup of tea and a bit of toast, will you have a cup?' she asked. 'Go on, it will do you good. I must remember to tell your Da those teeth are troubling you. You should have them out. Come on in.' she continued. 'No use you sulking out here. Come on,' she urged again. 'I'll put the teapot on, it'll be boiling in no time. I've coppers for the gas.'

I followed my Ma indoors, feeling more than a little sorry for myself. Over a cup of tea and a chat, we talked about my teeth and Guinness's Brewery, or rather their life-saving free dispensary.

'Why don't you walk down there now?' she said. 'And get your teeth seen to. Don't worry about another job just yet.'

The dispensary nurse examined my mouth and gave me a card. It was, in fact, an appointment card to a down-town clinic for the following week. I was to have an anaesthetic — in those days gas, which you breathed in while you held your hand skyward. When it dropped, you'd obviously had enough.

I was nervous when I arrived at the clinic and a quick glance around at the other seated people in the out-patients' department didn't allay my fears one little bit. Nervous bottoms were moving along well polished seats as names were called. Bodies vanished behind a green painted door, ushered in by a white-coated nurse. I noted with mounting alarm that all movement was inward, there seemed to be no one coming out.

'Perhaps there's another entrance,' my Ma said soothingly. She had accompanied me and I was glad of her comforting company, irrespective of the fact that she had to be present to sign the relevant papers giving her consent for the anaesthetic to be administered. Soon it was my turn to face the hidden terror behind the door.

The nurse called crisply, 'Purdy!'

'In you go,' my Ma said, giving me a nudge.

The nurse guided me by the shoulders gently through the door. A short walk along the corridor, through another door (a glass door this time) and there before my eyes all was revealed. The patients that had preceded me were all laid out on beds, sleeping it off. It was a relief to see them, bloody but well.

The gas was not as bad as I had expected. After a few snorts I could feel myself rapidly weakening. It seemed as if I was holding on to the back of a fast moving train, its shrill urgent whistle penetrating my brain as it raced towards the inky blackness of a tunnel. I was going to fall.

'Hold on, hold on!' a voice cried.

'I can't! I can't!' my scream mingled with a rush of steam. Suddenly blackness. Perfect indescribable blackness. Then I was awake spitting and struggling. I heard the dentist's voice, 'Easy boy, easy.'

He must have thought I was a horse. My face was slapped quite hard. That brought some semblance of sense to me. I was conscious now and aware of my senses. I could taste warm blood in my mouth, the holes left by the five stumps felt soft and mushy. My head was held over a dish and encouraging tones prompted me to part with my red spittle.

The next few days were very unpleasant, but soon my gums hardened. My speech remained odd. Some weeks elapsed before my false teeth were fitted. They were handsome, the latest thing in plastic. I had a weird feeling that my upper lip was a yard ahead of my face, but that feeling soon passed and thanks to Arthur Guinness I was a presentable young man again.

My next job was landed more by luck than energetic effort. I wasn't to be a messenger boy just yet. A young girl with whom I was acquainted worked at one of the two local laundries. One lunch hour, while showing off my newly acquired good looks, she happened to mention that the laundry — namely the White Heather in the South Circular Road — required a van boy. I decided to string along with her back to work. She went directly in to the steaming hot jungle of the Hoffman press shop. I idled outside — the office was still closed for dinner. Later I was told the position was mine — no shit, no reference, no nothing.

'When can you start?'

'Tomorrow.'

'Fine. You will start at twelve shillings and sixpence a week.' My heart bounded — Jaysus, twelve and a tanner!

My Ma was delighted when I gave her the good news. 'Better than the old bike; shorter hours too,' she intoned.

'It's only ten shillings a week, Ma,' I lied, faking disgust.

'What matter?' she replied. 'It's work, isn't it. And it will keep you off the street.'

Ma always ended on that note.

The laundry van was an open back affair. A tarpaulin was supplied to keep the newly cleaned laundry dry. The dirty linen could fend for itself. We had plenty of hampers or baskets for delivery to hotels and restaurants, some of which were quite heavy. The driver proved to be a hard taskmaster.

'The quicker the boy, the shorter the day,' he more than often argued. 'And the longer the evening too,' he would add. No doubt to shampoo his whiskers in lots of frothy pints.

New boys, of course, are always a little slower, not being able to anticipate the next customer, and so forth. After a couple of weeks, the boy would be more helpful. I soon got to know when we would have an easy day and vice versa.

One of our stops was the Tubercular Peamount Sanatorium. Large amounts of linen were collected from this tubercular hive. 'Germs Wednesday' I called it. I never discovered, try as I did, if the linen was from staff quarters or patients. I took an instant dislike to handling it, fearful of the disease and its consequences. This was long before the discovery of the wonder drug streptomycin, which was finally to cure the killer disease. On the way back to the laundry from Peamount, I would stand up in the back of the van rather than sit on what I termed 'contaminated linen'. Luckily, Peamount was our last call before finishing for the day. I had to lend a hand in unloading the van, a job which I also detested. It seemed I'd an aversion to dirty linen from sanatoriums.

The driver was hard to please, you had to be off the back of the van, running with the parcel before he came to a halt. A string of invective forever perched on his lips as an incentive to hurry you along. My ability to answer with equal and useful forcefulness didn't help. Soon he was calling me a lazy little bastard and I was referring to him as a shagging old pox. He didn't take too kindly to this and frequently insisted I was a foul-mouthed little cur. I couldn't really disagree with his findings but then I couldn't hold my tongue either. The end came when I was summoned to appear before the manager. He didn't beat about the bush, his tone was curt.

'The roundsman tells me you're cheeky and uncontrollable. I have no alternative but to dismiss you at once.'

I accepted the proffered pay packet. No week in lieu of notice, no holiday pay, just my twelve and a tanner. My Ma wasn't too pleased when I gave her the bad news, a van boy was a step higher than a messenger boy. Ma was a bit of a social climber on the quiet. The weekend was spent probing various sources for work. I was determined to get a start for Monday. That day saw me again at Rathmines, ambling from shop to shop, window to window. At last in the corner of a grocer shop was the little white card, 'MESSENGER BOY WANTED. APPLY WITHIN.' I did just that and got the job.

'Ten shillings a week, plus tips,' the owner said. 'And you get a wrap-up every Saturday night.'

To take home a wrap-up could vary from shop to shop, but basically it consisted of the left overs after the week's business was completed. Perishables that would not hold their freshness over 'til opening time the following Monday, ends and scraps of bacon and so on were part of the general contents of a food parcel. It always helped one's Ma. I know my Ma was glad to receive these handouts which not every shopkeeper issued. Sausages and bacon could be made into a coddle which was and indeed is, a very tasty dish. Water, flour and a little pepper and salt, plus a couple of onions were the extra ingredients required.

The messenger boy's lot was a hard one. His day started at nine o'clock Monday, Tuesday, Wednesday and Thursday. Friday and Saturday it was eight-thirty. Wednesday was generally early closing day at one o'clock, but often, very often, Friday and Saturday were marathons. Finishing time could be as late as the unholy hour of eleven-thirty. The other evenings the time was more or less an early six o'clock. One was usually allowed to take the bike home — big deal. I remained a messenger boy until I was fourteen. We were a sturdy lot and thieved what we could, when we could.

During these two years I worked at several different shops and it would be pedestrian from the reader's point of view to dissect each job and the weeks between. However, there are some points worthy of mention. The period was as real eye-opener for me and it brought home with startling clarity my true position in society. Lots of houses had servants and the accusing finger on a brass plate, generally fixed to a pillar, pointing to the tradesmen's entrance reminded you often of your lowly position in life. It certainly didn't boost your ego.

The shop sold every conceivable item that the well-stocked kitchen would require. Most shops had sawdust spread on the floor and behind the counter. The messenger boy's last chore would be to sweep up the spent sawdust and spread the new, ready for opening time.

The first week for any errand boy was low profile, that is if he was shrewd. To lead an honest altar boy existence was the norm. You kept your hands to yourself and touched nothing. Most shops laid a trap to test your integrity. Behind the counter, at sweeping-up time was normally the spot chosen to spring the trap. The bait was usually a ten shilling note, nestling on top of the sawdust. You could tell when you were up for grabs, if you had your wits about you. The assistants would vacate the area chosen, and head for the opposite side of the shop. Just like a mini Dunkirk they would flee, leaving you with the beach all to yourself. Naturally you handed the ten shillings over with a surprised look-what-I've-found countenance. There would be smiles all round, followed by a pat on the back and a chorus of 'Good boy!'

'He's a grand lad. Brought up right. You can always tell.'

'Nice young fellow, I could tell that from the start.' Etc., etc., etc....

The aftermath was, when you side-stepped the prepared trap, you considered yourself at liberty to steal, rob, lift and thieve. Of course, the penny would drop sooner or later, and you would be on the move again. I certainly never tired of the system. Neither did the shopkeepers.

The other hazardous part of the job was the tram tracks. Many a dive over the handlebars resulted from a wheel getting caught in the steel rails. The most trying time was when you still had a delivery in the basket. Eggs mingled with potatoes, flour, bacon, apples and Christ knows what else would scatter in all directions. Then taking the goods back to the shop for the inevitable ticking off and possibly the sack. The customer who ordered biscuits among other things became a prime target for pilfering. The bag containing the biscuits was always tied at the mouth with a small piece of cord. The tell-tale string was enough to invite closer inspection. Out of a pound of biscuits an average of three could be devoured without fear of detection.

The day dawned when I was caught in a way which surprised me. The biscuits concerned were fig rolls. I took two after stopping the bike to examine the contents of the delivery. Fig rolls are quite heavy, two was the limit. Having eaten these I continued merrily on my way to Rathgar. Arriving at my destination, I parked against the kerb. A middle aged woman answered the door to my knock. I duly handed over the box and was about to make my retreat when I heard her say: 'Wait a minute.'

I stopped and turned. 'Let's check the list,' she said matter of factly. It was then I noticed the small scales perched on the table just inside the door. Each item was ticked off the list as it emerged from the box. When the biscuits saw daylight they were promptly planted on the scales. I closed my eyes momentarily and held my breath.

'These biscuits are under-weight,' she intoned briskly. 'Take them back.'

I groaned at this suggestion. 'Have you interfered with the bag?' she asked curtly.

'No,' I stammered.

'Well, you've nothing to worry about have you?'

Taking the proffered biscuits from her hand I returned to my bike feeling guilty and despondent. My brain rolled for a solution to this unexpected problem. I didn't have any money, otherwise I'd have bought myself a quarter-pound and returned the two biscuits to the bag. That would have been the easy way. In the end though, I had to face up to it and take them back to the shop and face the music.

The scene in the shop was ugly. I strenuously denied all knowledge of the missing biscuits. The assistant was equally adamant that his scales were right and had given the proper weight. Something had to give in this impasse and that something was me. I was sacked on the spot. I blamed myself for this crass stupidity and pioneered future tactics for messenger boys. It was a simple manoeuvre and was adopted for all commodities whether biscuits, oranges, apples, pears, raisins or sweets. Every time I stopped to chat to another errand boy I passed on my solution. The goods stolen were not to be eaten until after the actual delivery had taken place. If the customer weighed the items and found them to be under-weight I would take them back to the shop but not before I'd returned the stolen goods to the relevant bag. This method led to various arguments between the customer and the assistant, each accusing the other of having faulty scales. Their faces were a study — snatching the packet from your hand, literally throwing it on the shop scales, their lips curled ready to give you a snorter, then dismay, utter dismay.

'Shagging old bitch, what is she on about, the poxy weight is right? What does she want? Tell her to blow off.'

In time one got to know every customer who checked the weight of goods delivered. Eventually, it was only a question of leaving these untouched.

Christmas was much looked forward to. Tips or Christmas boxes were plentiful and it didn't do to be a bad boy a month or so before the 25th. To be out of work then was insanity, pure and simple. There was a certain aura, a feeling of goodwill, fairy lights and decorations added to the uplifting of spirits.

The errand boy expected, and usually got, a double week's pay at Christmas, accompanied with a wrap-up. The hours worked that week were colossal. A fourteen hour day was commonplace. The extra week's pay was well earned. No over-time was paid — none whatsoever. The messenger bike would be so over-laden you were unable to ride it until the first two or three orders were delivered. The weight up front would be heavier than the kid sitting behind. You had to walk along the road with armpit pressed firmly onto the saddle to maintain the status quo. And the rain. The days when it really threw it down, especially the long and arduous days, Friday and Saturday. If it happened to rain all day Saturday, and more than occasionally it did, you would be wet through even before you reached work.

Oilskins for messenger boys were not on the agenda. There was a plentiful supply of sacks (most shops sold potatoes so there was no shortage of empty sacks). It was fashionable to drape a sack over your shoulder like a cloak, another over your head like a hood hanging down your back, a piece of string round the middle and a safety pin did the rest. After the delivery of half a dozen orders the sacks would be wet through, so you would change for dry ones. By this method you would stay just wet 'til around eleven. By lunch you would be soaked to the bone. The cycle home to lunch with a few orders to drop off on the way wouldn't help much. The dinner of sausage and pudding would be ready with a place reserved for you by the fire. This enabled you to dry out during the break. There just weren't any other dry clothes to change into. The steam would rise from your socks, draped across the hob; your shoes as near to the fire as possible. The legs of your trousers would also belch steam as you sat gulping bread and butter and drinking hot sweet tea.

The afternoons on these wet days were agony. Another nine or ten hours' toil lay ahead, and being half dry on your return to work, you would have to go through the process of getting soaked all over again. When this state of affairs was reached, you were then at the point of resignation. You couldn't get any wetter if you jumped into The Liffey; the consolation being, of course, that on the bike you at least wouldn't drown.

Saturday was pay day for the errand boy. The wage wouldn't be paid until the last order was safely delivered. On one such wet Saturday it seemed the oceans of the world had changed place with the sky and the mythical Noah's Ark would at any moment be a stark and terrible reality. The time was after eleven at night. I stood in the shelter of a porch at a house in Rathgar. The water that dripped from my clothes and sacks formed a pool at my feet that would have kept a nomadic tribe and fifty camels going for a month. It was my last delivery and the faint steps from within told me that someone was paying attention to my urgent request for the door to be opened. The large knocker, in the shape of a lion's head, hung black and perpendicular to the woodwork.

The door opened to reveal a tall thin lady, dressed in a red nightgown. She sported a large nose which stood out like a bow-sprit on some ancient sea-going vessel. She began to complain bitterly about my late arrival, she had been ready for bed for ages. I took the orders as they were given to me, but it seemed hopeless even trying to explain. I stood there like the idiot I was and let her get on with it. I thought for a minute she would simply take the box of groceries and slam the door. That would have suited me fine, but by now she was like an avaricious terrier with its teeth sunk deeply into its adversary. She was not letting go. If Mr so-and-so didn't appreciate her custom, then it would be taken elsewhere. The money spent in the grocer's shop was considerable and a little appreciation was expected in the service, which obviously wasn't forthcoming. I didn't even begin to try and placate her, I was all in. I just wanted to get back to the shop for my wages.

When her tongue ceased clacking her thin lips sealed tight under the awning that was her nose. She began, to my utter dismay, to check through the box of groceries, taking each item out and placing it on a table standing just inside the door. A white paper bag caused her to stare, her nose entered the bag to reappear haughtily.

'I didn't order this,' she cried with a huh! 'Cooked sliced ham. Cooked ham,' she repeated parrot fashion. 'What on God's earth is that doing in here?'

'Take it back,' she ranted.

I took the proffered bag. She rummaged further into the contents until satisfied that all the orders were present and correct, I turned wearily to leave, descending the steps which led down from her front door.

'Disgraceful! Young boys out at this hour of the night. In this weather too.' Her shrill voice followed me to the gate. That was her parting shot.

Once outside I looked closely at the sliced ham. I was ravenous and hadn't eaten since dinner hour. Taking a slice of ham from the bag I folded it neatly in half and slipped it into my mouth. Needless to say, it tasted delicious and out came another slice and another until the lot vanished in a mad moment of *Cordon Bleu* fantasy.

When I got back to the shop the owner was waiting to lock up, the assistants having gone home. I placed a basket with the empty boxes on the floor near the counter, I could see the four half crowns in a little heap, my wages for the week. I moved along the counter to collect. Normally I'd pick up the money and mutter a hurried 'Good night' and be on my merry way. When I reached the wages he said, 'Where's the ham?'

The suddenness and unexpected nature of the question stopped me dead in my tracks. I was dumbfounded. I expected the query when long nose got her bill, and had thought of it cycling back to the shop, but that would be another day, I'd reasoned, and pushed the thought from my mind. Now here I was being immediately confronted with its whereabouts.

'Well?' he intoned impatiently. 'I'm waiting. Where is the ham? Mrs Long Nose has been on the 'phone. She didn't order it and sent it back. Where is it?, he prompted, 'speak up.'

My eyes searched and my feet scratched and my brain wheeled for an answer to a question so bluntly put. There was only one answer, no excuses, the answer was a straight and simple one: the truth. The truth, I'd been told often enough, never hurt anyone. Those few kind words turned out to be the biggest load of rubbish I'd ever heard. My eyes looked to the floor, which had been swept clean, ready for the new sawdust, unable for the minute to look the boss in the eye. I straightened my wet shoulders with resignation, my eyes swivelled to meet his.

'I've eaten it,' I heard myself mutter.

'You've eaten it?' he glared back. 'The whole pound? Greedy little bastard,' he hissed. 'Where's the bike?'

'Outside,' I said dejectedly.

'Bring it in,' he snarled.

My movements were automatic as I carried out his instructions. Having placed the bike against the counter I again stood before him; contempt was all over his face.

'A pound of ham is one shilling and three pence,' he said gravely. 'Deduct one shilling and three pence from ten shillings.... Well, what does it leave?' he urged.

'Eight shillings and nine pence,' I said in a whisper, suddenly realising my fate.

Taking a half crown from the pile he went solemnly to the till and returned with the change. Handing me the remainder he snapped, 'Don't come in Monday morning. You're sacked and if you want to know why you're sacked — it's dishonesty.'

The door swung shut silently behind me. It was a quarter to midnight, still raining and a two mile walk home. There was a squelching noise coming from my shoes as I hurried homeward. Passing a fish and chip shop that was still open for business, I entered and bought four pennyworth of chips; they were brown and crispy. My pocket money had now dwindled to eleven pence. At least I still had me Ma's seven and a tanner.

I arrived home at Down Patrick Road at twenty minutes to one. The house was silent as I entered. The fire was almost out. The teapot on the hob contained warm tea. A couple of cuts of bread and a slice of Kraft cheese were laid out on a place for my supper. I poked the fire into life, adding a couple of sods of turf.

Removing my clothes, I noticed my feet were white and crinkly from continuous immersion in water. Wringing my socks out in the sink, I draped them on a chair along with my other clothes, pulling the chair as close to the fire as I dared. I gulped down the bread and cheese. The tea tasted stewed, but I wasn't fussy, and drank it greedily. Silently I mounted the stairs and entered the bedroom. The mattress tucked into the right-hand corner of the floor seemed inviting. Two of my brothers were already sleeping. I eased myself in, my cold feet gently making a passage between their still bodies. They stirred involuntarily, their movement sufficient to enable me to snuggle in comfortably. The day behind now seemed like a bad dream. The bliss of sleep crept up and overpowered my living senses.

# Chapter 10

Towards the age of fourteen I arrived home one evening. My mother's anxious voice greeted me. The news was bad.

'A detective has been here looking for you,' she said, giving me a 'what have you been up to' look. 'You haven't been lifting have you?' she queried.

'No Ma,' I answered without much conviction. 'What did he want?' I asked, trying to keep a steady voice.

'I don't know,' she replied. 'You've to report to the police station and see him as soon as you get in. He said it was just a few questions.'

Typical, I thought, racking my brain for answers that weren't there. I'd been lifting like all the other messenger boys, but this last week I'd been out of work and I only lifted from work, generally. So it was with mixed feelings that I made my way to the police station and asked to speak to a certain detective.

'Hang on there,' was the station sergeant's reply.

I watched as he disappeared into the office, returning presently with another giant of a man in plain clothes, who, without a shadow of a doubt, was a redneck.

'So you're Jim Purdy?' he grated rather unpleasantly. 'Follow me, I want to speak to you.'

I was ushered into a room: a sinister looking room with one single barred window. A bare electric light bulb hung from the ceiling on eighteen inches of flex. A table and two chairs were the only furniture. The plastered walls had been recently distempered and a square of linoleum covered the floor. An ashtray lay in the middle of the otherwise bare table.

We sat, inspecting each other across no man's land. He

smiled, showing a large set of teeth. Teeth that a tiger shark would have been proud of. His eyes were round and grey and cunningly peered from a 'short back and sides' head. Minutes lapsed before he spoke.

'Do ye smoke Jim?' he said at last. A question which took me completely off guard.

'I do,' I mumbled, showing a little dismay.

'All young lads smoke nowadays,' he continued, fetching a packet of Players from his pocket. 'Well, you would like one now I suppose?' He threw a smoke to my side of the table. I didn't have a butt on me and was grateful for the proffered cigarette.

'Tell me Jim, are you working?'

I replied in the negative.

'These are hard times for youngsters such as yourself, are they not? Plenty of work in England, though. Still, you're too young are you not? Tell me what your age is Jim?'

'Fourteen,' I said, puffing away at the fag like a veteran, by now feeling a little more relaxed.

'Tell me Jim, where did you work last?'

I replied with confidence, naming the shop. I'd nothing to hide by disclosing that, in fact, my last job paid fifteen shillings a week. Wages were rising and I actually terminated the job of my own accord after asking for and being refused a rise. Other jobs were paying seventeen shillings and sixpence and in some cases a whole pound. England was now a haven for employment. Lads of sixteen and seventeen were taking the plunge and leaving the Emerald Isle.

'So you left that job did you,' shark-mouth intoned. 'Why Jim?'

'I asked for more money,' I said, taking a last drag at the smoke which by now was reduced to a butt.

'And you didn't get a rise, did you Jim?'

'No,' I said flatly.

'Did you take any money by way of compensation?' he fired back.

'No I didn't,' I said, baulking at this sudden turn of events.

'I think you did,' he smirked. 'Tell me Jim, what did you spend it on, eh?'

'Spend what on sir?' I echoed incredulously.

'Now Jim, I've been nice to you haven't I?'

'I don't know what you're talking about sir,' I croaked. His burly frame rose from the chair.

'I'm going into the other room for a minute or two,' he said soothingly. 'You will make a full statement won't you Jim? You're a good lad, I can tell that. You come from a respectable home. I had a word with your mother, you succumbed to temptation, that's it Jim, isn't it? Make a full statement like a good lad before I come back. Just repay the money, that's all you have to do. Not another word will be said about it. Then you can go home, back to your pals. Sure they'll be wondering where you are, and you don't want to be here all night do you? Of course you don't.'

Leaving a pencil and blank sheet of paper on the table, he left the room. Alone now, I sat there unable to comprehend; bewildered, puzzled and scared. Minutes ticked by. The silence was eerie. I heard the door click open as shark-mouth re-entered. I'd written nothing on the sheet of paper. Shark-mouth was angry now and tried a different tack.

'Well?' he asked sternly. 'You made no statement?'

'No,' I replied, with some misgiving.

I saw his arm rise and curve back, bringing it down in an arch he slapped my face sharply with his open hand.

'Perhaps that will help you remember.' My face smarted under the impact.

'What am I supposed to have done sir?' I began.

'You stole five pounds from your last employer,' he spat, commencing to unfold an amazing chronicle of events.

Shark-mouth had undoubtedly done his homework. It transpired that when he called at my Ma's he extracted from her a list of names and addresses of my pals — three in all. He called on each of them in turn and was now in possession of three rather damning statements taken from each with the connivance of their parents. As stated previously, I was no angel but the events leading up to this confrontation are certainly worth relating.

The preceding week, while walking the streets looking for work, I happened to spot a lady's purse which was sitting sedately on top of a pram, with a gurgling happy baby just below the blankets. The pram was parked on a footpath which led to the door of a well-to-do house. The temptation was great. I was stony broke. The purse was soon in my grasp and I was lamming it down the road, each stride taking me further away from the scene of the crime.

Stopping at the first opportunity, I examined the contents. The purse contained three pound notes and ten shillings in silver. A fortune by any standard — for me anyway. This money I gladly spent and shared with my pals, with trips to the pictures and the skating rink. My skating was confined to a little annexe off the main rink known as Mug's Alley. Cigarettes, fish and chips and chocolate were in abundance, while the dough lasted.

Well fed for a week — for that's about the length of time it had taken to spend the lot — I'd told my pals about the source of our deliverance and they didn't seem to care one way or another; a good time was all that mattered.

My late employer, who was a personal friend of the detective, happened to mention in passing conversation that five pounds was missing from his shop. It wasn't an official complaint. This money went missing during my brief but otherwise honest period of employment. The first I'd heard of the missing money was on that unforgettable evening at the police station. However, shark-mouth had delved further into the business of the missing money, and on learning that a messenger boy had recently deserted his position became more interested and asked the proprietor to make it an official complaint. As messenger boys did most of the lifting it was reasonable to assume that I'd taken the money. I was dumbfounded with this mass of damning evidence. Shark-mouth, with equal assumption, considered the case cut and dried. The horror of it all unfolded before my very eyes. My position seemed hopeless, yet I still strenuously denied lifting the five pounds.

'And all the money you spent on your pals — where did that

come from, my little gossoon? Tell me that will you?'

The redneck had me by the scrotum, and he knew it. I still wouldn't sign a statement and took the only other alternative, informing him somewhat meekly that I'd found the money. He looked at me derisively.

'I've a good mind to give you another one in the lug, you lying little bugger.: I'll see you cry for mercy before Judge McCarthy,' he warned.

My heart skipped a beat at the mention of McCarthy. Judge McCarthy struck fear into the bowels of any wayward Dublin children. McCarthy has since departed this life and I sincerely hope he's enjoying a warmer climate. I was duly charged with theft before being allowed home. My esteemed pals were not implicated with charges of accessory after the fact.

The day arrived for the hearing and with it came fear and trepidation. The Judge was duly seated. The Court was crowded with Dublin's juvenile delinquents. The charge was read with power and gusto by shark-mouth. My pals were all present, accompanied by their mothers, as I was. They soon said their little piece. I could feel my liberty slipping away. One after another they nervously related my apparent generosity. I stood up front by the bench, scrubbed clean for the occasion. Judge McCarthy looked at me gravely.

'And you still deny taking this money,' he asked.

'Yes sir,' I replied without conviction.

'Well, the circumstantial evidence is overwhelming,' he intoned. 'I find you guilty as charged.'

The face of shark-mouth flushed. His fangs were exposed in a grin of apparent satisfaction.

'James Purdy, you'll go to Dangain Reformatory for two years.'

Two years … the words echoed. Two whole shagging years for a lousy five pounds. I could feel the blood deserting my face like the sand from an egg timer. But cry … no. The shagging redneck wouldn't get that satisfaction. My Ma was on her feet in a flash, strongly protesting at such a severe sentence.

'I'll pay the five pounds,' she implored.

'He won't admit to the crime,' the Judge said solemnly.

I stood there pale, uneasy, bewildered, shocked. A short whispered discussion took place on the bench, another redneck approached and held my arm, ready to take me below. McCarthy cleared his throat.

'I'll retract that sentence,' he said. 'You will go to the remand centre at Marlborough House for one week. Time to think it over, so to speak, and if you haven't decided to tell the truth by then,' he warned sternly, 'the original sentence stands.'

I felt myself being tugged by the sleeve, the redneck had me in a firm grip leading me away.

I arrived at Marlborough House in a 'hurry-up waggon'. Two other kids who were also remanded sat by my side. It was a late wintry Friday afternoon. The holding room below the Court had been a nightmare of screaming terror from children, echoing strong and urgent pleas; seeking the solace and comfort of their mothers. Some off to Artane, others off to County Offaly, to the horror and confines of Dangain.

Marlborough House was large and Victorian, surrounded by a formidable wall. It was run by a married couple — a matron-come-cook and her spouse who was the watchman. We were ushered into a rather large dormitory where we would spend the days playing snakes and ladders, ludo and draughts.

We were just in time for tea. Now that the initial shock was over, I could feel the pangs of hunger. I hadn't eaten since break-fast that morning, which had been the usual fried bread and tea. At the Centre we sat down almost immediately on forms pushed against long wooden tables which seated approximately fifty children. The bread was brought round on a large tray by a plump kindly woman. We had a side plate and a giant mug. Each kid was invited to take two cuts. If you were sitting at the top of the table your choice was obviously two big cuts. I being a new boy, soon realised why the mad charge for positions had taken place. There was jam on the bread, thinly spread and scattered over a large area. His nibs, our guardian and watchman, followed with a large pot with an even larger spout. Our mugs were filled with shell cocoa. This foul smelling and foul tasting liquid is made from the actual shell of the cocoa bean. It was a horrible drink. That and my two small cuts of bread left a void. Although I could have eaten more bred, I wasn't anxious for more cocoa.

Lots of kids present were in bare feet and ill-fitting clothes. After tea we all helped to clear up, wipe down the tables, sweep the floor. There weren't many crumbs about. The time was then our own until eight o'clock. I spent the next two hours trying to get a smoke, moving from group to group, game table to game table. One youngster offered me a piece of paper.

'Fold it up tight,' he said, 'you'll get a drag out of it.'

With this bit of information I edged nearer to the turf fire, first having folded the paper in the shape of a cigarette. Nelson's eye was the watchman's response, he turned the other way as I got down on my hunkers to extract a light from the glowing ember of turf. Strangely enough, it didn't taste too bad. I would now have to get myself some paper and immediately began a quiet search of the dormitory. There wasn't a comic or a book in sight, not even a Bible. No doubt they'd all gone up in smoke.

Bedtime was at the early hour of eight o'clock. Prior to this confined stay I don't remember ever having to retire at such an unearthly hour. We were herded single file towards the stairs; these led to a large corridor. Seats lay along the wall of the landing. We had to strip naked here and fold our clothes neatly in piles. Our nightshirts hung down from a hook in line with our civvies. They were all the same length, so it didn't matter which one you chose. Pulling it over my head, I realised it was another first. I had never worn night clothes before. I somehow felt like a cissy.

I stood back whilst the other kids went to their respective beds. There were plenty of vacant ones. Soon I was between crisp white sheets, with a bed all to myself — pure luxury. I went to sleep almost immediately. I awoke once or twice, realising I was in a strange place, but soon fell asleep again without much trouble.

Early the following morning saw me standing before a long line of cold water taps with some half bars of Sunlight soap strewn along the trough. We washed quickly, not dilly-dallying, the water was far too cold. Breakfast was served shortly after we dressed. More shagging shell cocoa, another two cuts of bread, this time with a scraping of margarine.

The day was long and boring. Us kids mostly talked about our own problems.

'I didn't do it, cross my Jaysus heart.'

'My word of honour. Honest I didn't. I'll get two years, I know I will.'

'This is my first time before Mac.'

'Artane for Peddar, he done three gas meters. He could hardly carry the Jaysus pennies, bound to be nabbed.'

Recreation time was ten to half past. A field on the north side of the building was the venue, football the game. Coats were removed and goal posts formed. The ball was ceremoniously thrown onto the pitch by the watchman — it was a ball made of rags. To kick it in between a pair of coats lying on the ground was, if not impossible, most certainly highly improbable. I didn't even try; just merely jogged along the fringe of the howling mob. This was purgatory, two years of this would drive me bonkers. I vowed there and then to tell his lordship that I'd lifted the five pounds. Aye, and do a bit of grovelling into the bargain. As my brother used to say, when you get through the sole of your boots, you'll be back on your feet. Judge McCarthy would find before him a nice well-mannered bundle of innocence.

When this charade of soccer was over we were ushered back inside the dormitory to await dinner. I latched on to one character named Boxer. He had done a little bit of amateur scrapping and used to prance about the dormitory shadow boxing, his thin arms punching the empty space, his nose making heavy snorting noises, for effect no doubt. It seemed to work because Boxer always sat at the head of the table and always seemed to have plenty of bits of paper to roll and smoke. Boxer, though, was only twelve, I was fourteen. Age was then a great advantage. I had also been working for a couple of years, which was a great boost to my standing with the others. In short, I was classed as a 'big fellow'. The name 'big fellow' held a certain status. He who worked was in a class of his own. Actually, my height was five feet two inches then. In the next four years I would grow to six feet.

When dinner was served, Boxer assured me of a place by his side. The word went round double quick and sure enough a space next to Boxer was left vacant for my exclusive use. I was grateful for my position next to Boxer.

'It doesn't count for much,' Boxer said.

'I thought it did,' I countered, with a note of disappointment. The short, grubby, freckled, skinny face of Boxer turned in my direction.

'Not Saturday. It's only Irish Stew. One ladleful is all you get with a cut of dry bread; real watery too. It's Jaysus terrible. A shagging pig would turn his nose up at it.'

Sure enough Boxer was right. I could see a piece of carrot doing a duet with half a potato. There were also plenty of frogs eyes glaring at you from the surrounding area. Boxer dunked his bread in and was soon slurping down his first mouthful. I didn't need any prompting as to where my bread should go.

'Is there anything else after this?' I asked Boxer between mouthfuls.

'Of course there Jaysus is,' Boxer replied.

'What?' I asked hopefully.

'Grace after meals,' he said. 'Where do you think you are? You're not going to tell me you get sweet at home?'

'No,' I replied, 'only Sundays,' feeling the fool I was.

Sunday afternoon was visiting time. Very few kids received visitors. I happened to be one of the lucky ones. My Da arrived about four o'clock. The front room was set aside for such purposes: it was small and well furnished; two armchairs and a sofa, a couple of straight backed chairs tucked under a round mahogany table. My father in his Sunday best was already seated in one of the armchairs when I was ushered in. There were no other visitors present, my father had left it a bit late. We eyed each other in silence. Finally I found my tongue.

'Did you bring any smokes Da?'

'No I didn't,' came his stern reply. 'I told you many times before, you're too young to be smoking. This will do you more good,' sliding a bar of chocolate in my direction. I slipped the bar of Cadbury's Milk into my pocket.

'How are they treating you?'

I told him about the shell cocoa.

'What do you expect, champagne?'

'Have you finished with the paper?' I asked, noticing it sticking out of his pocket.

'More or less,' he croaked, tugging it clear of his jacket. I quickly pushed it under my jersey, straightening it out as I did so to lessen the chance of a bulge. There was an abhorrent silence, neither of us spoke for several minutes. Finally my Da spoke.

'When you got back in front of McCarthy on Friday, tell him you stole the money.'

'Your Ma and I will raise it by then,' he continued. 'Anyway, you should have admitted it before now and saved us all this bloody trouble.'

I opened my mouth to protest but thought better of it. Taking the wrapper off the chocolate I began to eat it. I reasoned that if Boxer clapped an eye on it he would demand half, at least!

'Are you listening?' my Da repeated.

I nodded in the affirmative. The door opened; visiting time was over. My Da seemed relieved to be going. 'Good luck,' he called, without as much as a backward glance.

I found myself in the dormitory, surrounded by a swarm of howling kids, all demanding to know what presents I'd received, if any. Boxer was elbowing his way through the mob.

'Make way there. Out of it. Vamoose, scram. Go on get out. All right Jim?' He reached my side protectively. 'Who was it? Your Da? Did he bring you anything?'

I flashed him the concealed paper. 'Jaysus,' he exclaimed with delight. 'A whole newspaper. We'll have smokes for a week. Not a word to anyone, you hear.'

All the other kids had already seen it anyway.

'Come on. Let's get to the fire and have a drag before tea. What paper is it?' Boxer queried.

'*Sunday Independent*,' I whispered.

'*Sunday Independent*,' Boxer whistled. 'Jaysus, we'll be

smoking like a power station.'

And so the week passed between rag football, paper smokes and shell cocoa. It was a horrible week that stood out against all other horrible weeks which had made up the first fourteen years of my life. Friday arrived none too soon, the day of reckoning. My mouth was dry from smoking newspaper and wondering how Judge McCarthy would react to my belated confession. I still didn't know what I was going to say and had turned various statements over in my mind. They all seemed inadequate.

'Purdy!" My name was called by the watchman. 'Your car is here.' There was a note of sarcasm in his voice. I made my way to the waiting paddy wagon. It was an ordinary police car this time doing the ferrying back to the court. I was alone. I'd said my goodbyes to Boxer, who was due to appear the following Monday.

We left the detention centre block behind and headed for the city. The morning was sunny. Most of the places we passed were new to me — not exciting, just interesting. Many thoughts swirled in my head. Would the Judge be in a good mood? It was Friday, that was a good sign. Everybody was happy on Friday — why should McCarthy be the exception? My fingers were crossed, superstition was rife. Banshees, goblins and fairies, touch wood, it all helped if your nerves were having a hard time.

The traffic snarled up at Capel Street Bridge. This part of the city I was well acquainted with. We hadn't far to go. Dublin Castle was just across the bridge, a formidable and imposing building. It was used for various government functions besides dealing with juvenile delinquents.

The car swung into the vast courtyard. The palms of my hands were damp with sweat. I could see my Da waiting at the entrance. He'd had to have a day off work which undoubtedly wouldn't help the budget and all this for a 'not guilty' conscience.

It was almost mid-day before I was brought from below to face my tormentor. A week had passed which was as distasteful a one as I'd ever had, and another one hundred and three of the same would amount to almost a week for every missing shilling.

My name was called, my Da patted my head as I made my nervous way forward to stop within three feet of the Judge.

McCarthy busied himself with some papers on the bench, never once looking in my direction. Minutes passed, fast heart-beating minutes. Mac seemed to be deep in thought. He was paying particular attention to one piece of paper, he held it in his left hand and sifted through other papers with his right. I could see his eyes swivel to and fro at regular intervals. Finally, satisfying himself that all was well, he stacked the sheets of paper together. His head shifted slowly from the downward position. He was now looking at me directly. It was a very indifferent look too, that much I was aware of. My mouth felt dry again and the tide was ebbing from my face. Eternity came and went before he spoke.

'I have given you one week to give me an honest answer.' The voice was curt. 'Did you or did you not steal the five pounds?'

I tried to swallow but couldn't. Oh for a drink of water.

'Well?'

'Yes sir, I did,' I blurted it all out at once.My voice sounded odd and faint.

'Why didn't you admit this charge last week?'

'I would have done sir. I'm sorry, I was frightened sir.'

'You were frightened?' Mac echoed. 'Two years in Dangain frightened you didn't it?'

'Yes sir,' I readily agreed.

'Well Mr Purdy,' the Judge addressed my Da. 'This sum of money will have to be repaid.'

'I have the money here sir,' my Da said at once, flourishing a five pound note.

This was a real sacrifice on my parent's behalf. The implications of getting together such an amount struck a chord of disbelief and horror into my thin frame. The money was taken from my Da and passed across the bench. Shark-mouth was present and grinning with obvious delight. Another brilliant case cracked no doubt. The redneck bastard I thought, feeling the colour rush back to my cheeks, realising my release was imminent.

I got a long and deliberate dressing down from the Judge. His warning descended over my head like some grey cloud of smoke. Sheer and utter relief swept through me as I emerged from the Court — 'Free'. I walked with my Da to the bus stop, neither of us spoke. A number 50 bus soon came into view bound for Crumlin. As it ground to a halt he said simply, 'Let that be a lesson to you.'

The words struck home. I learned the lesson the hard way.

Within a week I was back in the saddle. This time more care and attention was given to details, each job I acquired was my first. Still only fourteen, it was easy to deceive the managers and proprietors with the information that I'd just left school. No reference was then required or asked for. I had by now taken an alias and changed it with each successive job. With a false name and address it became easy to lift and steal, a feat I undertook with a keen sense of dedication. The five pounds was soon repaid with interest, and I hope many a redneck spent many a foot-slogging day trying to solve the petty crimes I left in my vengeful wake.

During this period there appeared large and colourful posters depicting a smiling soldier flanked on either side by the tricolour and in big white letters the cry 'Join the Free State Army'. This was a time when England was draining the youth of Ireland with offers of instant employment, tales of exorbitant wages easily earned were being washed back across the water. Fifty pounds a week was bandied about in open-mouthed wonder.

'Jaysus, he was only over there two months, back here with a new suit and all, buying gargle for the whole pub. Terrible decent.'

The details were magnified as the blarney took hold of a nation so long deprived of a regular wage. The work was undoubtedly a fact as the UK shook itself, like a wet dog, from the debris of Hitler's bombs. The nation had to be rebuilt, and no better man than Paddy. Tales of large, inflated wage packets were not to be taken seriously, but if you did want work, well then you went for your life. All that was needed was the fare across the water, plus a week's lodging money. England's landladies it seemed had a nasty habit of asking for it in advance.

Desertion from the Irish Free State Army was reaching alarming proportions, hence the large advertising posters which adorned billboards on many a vacant plot. As young kids during the War, we used to follow the Irish soldier, especially if he was taking his girl out to the pictures. We normally moved in, looking for a bit of fun and a chase, and would saunter up behind the unsuspecting rookie and holler loudly — 'Ireland's only hope' — keeping up the cry at regular intervals, until the poor soldier would be goaded into giving chase, very often sparks flying from his boots as he wheeled in hot pursuit. Frequently it didn't work out in the way we intended. Lots of them took it in good sport, and merely laughed as they continued on their way, arm in arm with the girl of their choice.

Well, if the army had ever used the lads, it was now the turn of the lads to use the army. The short and simple answer was — join up for a couple of weeks, save your pay and you'll see the UK. The boots and slacks and greatcoat came in very handy on a building site. The pay of a private soldier then was twenty-seven shillings a week. Pay day for the army was Wednesday. A one way ticket on a steamer to Liverpool could be bought for fifteen shillings, so really all one needed was about four pounds.

The messenger boy's job was becoming dull and uninspiring. The extra ten shillings a week paid in the army (all found too) was more of a challenge — food to my ever changing moods. I had in the past delivered groceries to the officers' married quarters and at times would sidle into the privates' dining hall to bum a dinner. This request was never refused, but now in all seriousness, I was wondering if I could get away with it. Join up. Say I was eighteen (eighteen being the minimum age). I could send my Ma ten shillings a week and still have seventeen shillings left. The more I thought of it the more enthusiastic I became. The minimum height for entry was five feet two inches. I asked a pal to measure me standing erect against a lamp post. He informed me eagerly: 'You'll make it.' That settled it. My mind was made up. I'd take the plunge.

The owner of the shop where I worked then was a bible puncher. His first question every Monday morning was, 'Did you attend Mass yesterday, Tim?' (Timothy Burke was my current alias.)

'Yes, Mr Bible,' I'd reply, and I wouldn't be lying either, because I never missed Mass in those days. Yet here I was working under an assumed name and address, lifting all I could, when I could. Christ, wasn't I a perfect hypocrite!

It was now Friday, God bless it. I'd already decided to jack it in that week and try for the army on the Monday. I connived to get my wages on the Friday rather than Saturday, but the boss was not having any of it — to begin with, that is. I kept up the pressure and the lies poured out one after another. Finally he relented when I told him my Da had gone to England to get work and my Ma hadn't heard a word from him since.

'That's terrible,' he said thoughtfully., 'How long is he over there?'

'Two months, sir, and my Ma needs a few things. A few things in for the weekend,' I pleaded. My face was the picture of saintly innocence.

'I dare say she does, the poor woman. Some men have no heart at all.' He sighed, almost in tears, handing over seventeen shillings and sixpence.

'Thanks, Mr Bible,' I said, and set about delivering the early orders. Lunchtime approached. I loaded the groceries, those I'd normally deliver on my way home to dinner. Vengeance is mine said the Lord. That day I felt closer to his nibs than ever. Four large orders were now safely in the basket. I cycled straight home. My mother was terrified when I planted the lot on the kitchen table. Packets of bacon, butter, sugar, tea, flour and raisins were some of the goods. My Ma quickly donned her coat and fled the house in a state of panic, obviously expecting the rednecks to have the house surrounded. Nothing, it seemed, would calm her frayed nerves. My Ma never encouraged any lifting and would rather face an empty plate than have the rednecks besiege her home. My Da, too, with his respectable job in The Guinness Brewery, didn't encourage theft in any shape or form. I had different ideas and was certainly a difficult customer to handle at the best of times.

'An odd ball,' my mother used to say ruefully. 'I don't know who you take after,' despair clearly to the fore.

I raced the bike back to the shop which was still closed for lunch and parked it outside the door — here it would be seen. That was to be my last job as a messenger boy. In my own tin-pot way I reckoned I'd scored a victory over the slavery that existed. I seemed to get a deep and lasting satisfaction from this last act. A profound peace of mind purged my body from hate that had existed over the previous two years. I hopped on a bus, leaving 'the scene of the crime', as they say, behind me. Aye, behind me for ever. My lifting days were over. I never had the urge to thieve again and I never did. The goods I took home didn't do my Ma any good. The worry was there. Every knock on the door was a nerve racking experience and the sight of a redneck brought on an urge to visit the toilet. Still, we ploughed through it and I'm sure she breathed more freely when the cupboard was bare.

# Chapter 11

Portobello Barracks looked big and spacious as I approached the gates. I refrained that morning from using water (known as corporation hair oil) to plaster down my hair. A tousled head of hair made me look that little bit older and I hoped, too, that it would help me with the problem of my height. I was still only five feet two inches, no more no less. I didn't really expect to get any further than the sentry who I could see passing slowly to and fro. Another worry was my pubic hair. It had just started to sprout beneath my shirt. I looked very much like the fourteen years I was. God how I wished I was sixteen, it would have made matters so much easier.

I walked through the gate unchallenged, the sentry merely gazed at me with idle curiosity. I knew where the recruiting office was situated and walked on with all the aplomb I could muster. A corporal was busy at a desk. He glanced in my direction. My heart pounded realising it was now or never.

'Can I help?' he asked, looking me over and chewing on his pencil.

'I'd like to join up,' I said with as much calm as I could instil into my quaking body. My eyes avoided his and I tried to show casual interest in my surroundings.

'In there,' he pointed to another room. 'The sergeant will be back in a jiffy.'

The stream of invective I'd expected was not forthcoming. Christ, it can't be that easy, I thought, making swiftly for the room indicated, expecting any minute to hear a shout of, 'Stop you little impostor.' The jiffy turned out to be half an hour. I sat with increasing apprehension on a wooden chair looking at a measuring stick fixed to the wall, knowing if I survived the preliminaries I'd have to stand tall against its tell-tale inches for my height to be recorded. My mind wandered back to early that morning when I told my Ma I was off to join the army.

'At your age?' she gasped. 'You're joking, aren't you? God Almighty,' she continued, 'now I've heart everything! You a soldier — God protect us! Wait 'til your father hears this.'

The chafing reached a climax. Finally I stormed from the house slamming the door as I went, determined not to return. I would sleep rough that evening if the army rejected me. The year was 1948. I decided to keep the day and the month of my birth merely changing the actual year — easier to memorise — 1930 now taking precedence over 1934. If a birth certificate was required the game was up. One of my older brothers Brian was already in the army, using his certificate was out of the question. The eldest brother being six years older than me would have made my age twenty so that channel of thought was blocked for obvious reasons. Hearing footsteps in the outer office I hastily set fire to my last smoke, an act to steady my nerves and, hopefully, make me appear more of an adult. The door opened to show a military man, a three striper. I stood up.

'Good morning, sergeant,' I began, acutely aware of his close scrutiny. His eyes told me that he knew I was a fugitive from the cradle. He sat down heavily and sorted out a form from a bundle on his desk.

'So you want to be a free stater?' he cracked.

'Yes,' I replied, deciding to say as little as possible. Putting answers to questions was the name of the game. There was a time to act clever and a time to act dumb.

'I won't ask for your age,' he spoke with a hint of resignation. 'You're eighteen, right?'

'Yes sir.'

'Unhappy home?' he queried.

'Could be better sir,' I hedged.

'Name?' he asked, dipping the pen in ink.

'James Purdy,' I heard the pen scratching across the form.

'Date of birth?'

'Twenty fifth of March nineteen thirty.' The form was gradually filled, much to my satisfaction.

'When he'd finished he studied the form, deep in thought. Finally he proclaimed, 'It's up to the doctor. If he says "aye", you're in. But I'm afraid you'll have a long wait. He won't see you 'til this afternoon. Could be another half a dozen recruits besides yourself by then.' My hopes brightened at this suggestion. What better cover than to mingle with other 'recruits'?

'Just stay put,' the sergeant ordered leaving the room. So far, so good. No birth certificate asked for either. What luck! I felt more and more confident as the morning wore on. I paced up and down the small room, pausing only when the door opened in the outer office, to listen intently and hope it was another recruit. Someone else to talk to would have helped my edgy nerves. Boots stamped in and boots stamped out all morning, but not a civvy among them. Lunchtime came and the corporal I spoke to earlier entered.

'Go and get yourself a dinner.' He pointed towards the mess, a place which I knew well. The dinner was salted pork, with jacket potatoes and carrots, followed by a stodgy dish of sago. Having eaten my fill I wasted no time in hurrying back to the recruiting office, not wanting to be recognised. My face was familiar in the Rathmines area and I already knew a couple of regulars so I wasn't about to tempt fate at this stage. I was stony broke. A penny is little but a penny I didn't have. Being devoid of funds was nothing new however. I was not unduly worried. Another packet of smokes, though, would have been most welcome.

About half past two it happened, another recruit arrived. Much to my delight he didn't look all that old. In fact, it transpired he was seventeen. We exchanged tit-bits of information.

'You're not eighteen,' he said with conviction.

'Neither are you,' I replied with equal confidence.

'I bet I'm a lot older than you, though,' he parried.

'So what?' I barked feeling angry.

The conversation ceased abruptly as the sergeant entered to go through the same rigmarole. The new recruit said his name was Thomas Jefferson, from Tallaght. I listened with interest as the details were written down. When the sergeant had departed Tom produced a packet of smokes. My lucky star shines today, I thought, eyeing the packet from the corner of my left eye. The upsurge of spirits was soon dashed when he lifted the lid to reveal a single solitary cigarette.

'Sorry,' he said reading my thoughts, Placing the smoke between his lips he flung the empty packet to the floor.

'That's all right,' I said bitterly disappointed, My eyes looked longingly at the empty packet of Capstan Full Strength.

'Got a light?' Tom asked.

'I've plenty of matches,' I declared, producing a box of Pattersons.

'No dough?' Tom asked, blowing smoke in my direction.

'No. Skint,' I said. 'Haven't a tosser.'

'Same here. Don't get paid for the first fortnight in this outfit you know?' Tom said.

'News to me,' I replied.

'Shagging true, though.'

'Jaysus,' I cried. 'What will we do for a smoke?'

'Fuck knows,' said Tom, adding, 'Maybe the other lads will help us out, we can borrow a bob or two.'

'Yes,' I said hopefully.

'I hope so too,' said Tom. 'Anyway you're not in yet,' he reminded me. 'About time the quack got here, isn't it? Almost half three.'

Tom hardly got the words out of his mouth before the door opened. Framed in the doorway was an officer. The doctor had arrived. We both got to our feet hurriedly. The doc's face looked a bit flushed. He had a drop taken for sure. No doubt the Officers' Mess was the watering hole. He spoke kindly, hardly giving Tom and me a second glance.

'Only a brace today,' he offered. 'Business is bad, lads. I'm not earning my keep. Right then, who is first?'

I stepped forward.

'Over here.' He beckoned me to the measuring stick. I stood straight pushing my back against the apparatus and easing myself ever so slightly on to my toes. The stick landed on my head. I waited with bated breath.

'Just made it,' the doc's voice rang out. 'You're five feet two and a half inches. Now let me see you are …'

'Purdy,' I said hurriedly.

'Ah yes,' he said sorting one form from the other. 'Now strip to the waist,' he ordered, opening a small black satchel. My shirt was off before his stethoscope was around his neck.

'Breath in. Hold it. Breath out. In again. Sounds okay. Drop your trousers.' Down they went to my ankles. I was feeling rather foolish and inadequate.

'Cough.'

I complied. 'Again. You'll do,' he said going back to the form. He marked 'fit' in the appropriate place. The magic words were ringing in my ears, my trousers were back up to my waist in seconds. Tom's turn next. He was also pronounced fit. It was all over in ten minutes. The doctor paused at the door before departing.

'Of course, you know this is only the preliminary examination. A far more extensive medical awaits you at the Curragh Camp.' And with that, he was gone.

I turned to Tom with jubilation, 'Did you hear that?' I echoed. 'We're going to the Curragh.'

'Big Jaysus deal,' Tom said sarcastically.

'I've never been outside Dublin in my life,' I enthused. 'It'll be great, Tom.'

'Speak for yourself,' Tom replied thoughtfully, adding, 'I noticed one thing about you, Purdy.'

'What?' I said going on the defensive.

'You've no hair around your chestnuts.'

'What's that got to do with going to the Curragh?'

'Ah, you're only a Jaysus kid.' I blushed slightly at this remark because I'd noticed and was well aware of the black forest surrounding Tom's marriage tackle.

'The doctor said nothing,' I reiterated angrily.

'Why should he? You'll never handle the recoil of a rifle. A 303 will dislocate your shoulder, that's if it doesn't break your jaw first.'

'I'm willing to take the chance, so don't worry your little head about it.'

'I bet you don't last a month.'

'How much do you want to bet?' I challenged.

'Half a quid.'

'Right. You're on,' I replied.

By four o'clock the sergeant was back. He glanced at the forms. 'Both fit,' he said, grinning. 'Now to swear you in.'

Opening the drawer he fished out a large white card. 'Repeat the words after me,' he said solemnly.

We both complied rapidly with this request and vowed the Oath of Allegiance. 'Welcome to the fold,' he said when he'd finished, fishing a twenty packet from his pocket. 'I suppose you could do with one of these?' holding the packet in the air.

'Jaysus, gasping,' said Tom, taking one from the packet. 'I'd only one left coming in.'

'Yes, I see the remains on the floor,' the sergeant barked. 'Your empty packet?' he asked.

'Aye,' Tom replied.

'Aye,' the sergeant mimicked. 'You address me as Sir, Jefferson — understand?'

'Yes sir,' Tom said, visibly taken aback.

'Now pick up that packet and put it in there,' the sergeant said pointing to a wastepaper bin. 'We won't have any of your slovenly civvie habits in this man's army. Smoke, Purdy?'

'Yes sir, thank you,' I said puckering my lips. It was badly needed.

'Right, you two, at four-thirty get your lazy arses over to the Mess for tea, a lorry will be along presently to take you to the Curragh. It calls at two other recruiting posts first, this is its last call. Probably be about seven before it arrives. When you've had your tea get back here smartly and don't move. Got that?'

'Yes sir,' we both said in unison.

'Very well, have a pleasant journey. Do what you're told and you'll have no worries.'

'Thank you sir,' we called out as he departed.

Tom waited 'til the sergeant's footsteps faded before letting loose a stream of invective. 'Jaysus, that's a good start isn't it?' he moaned.

'Ah, he's not bad,' I replied. 'Gave us a fag didn't he?'

'Big deal!' Tom snorted. 'Not five minutes in the poxy outfit and he wants me to clean up the whole shagging barracks.'

'Ah, come on. It's nearly teatime. Let's see what's brewing. We made our way over to the Mess and took a seat at the back of the hall. The large tables were already laid out by the orderlies. A quarter of a loaf with a knob of butter perched on top, lay on a side plate with a fair helping of scrambled egg, a large mug of tea too. An excellent meal, ample and filling. I related my feelings to Tom.

'Good swag.' Tom agreed, but he was still smarting from the ticking off he'd received.

For me the only thing that marred an otherwise perfect day was the acute lack of funds. The night closed in quickly and darkness descended; it was getting quite cold. We were still waiting for the transport to arrive. The Curragh is thirty miles from Dublin. The journey, thankfully, would not be more than an hour's drive. Tom was becoming more and more dissident as the minutes wore on.

Finally, the wagon rolled up, it was seven-thirty. A corporal collected our papers and hurried us over the tailboard of the canvas covered truck. When my eyes became accustomed to the gloom I counted ten including Tom and myself. The duty corporal climbed up front with the driver, warmer there no doubt. I remember being well pleased at the large number of recruits. I wasn't so conspicuous amongst a crowd.

The engine revved into life, a short drive to the gate which by now was closed. A torch was shone into the back of the lorry by the guard commander. I blinked as it passed across my eyes. Not a word was spoken by anyone. An order was sounded to open the gate and we were on our way. Suddenly everyone began talking at once. The truck trundled down Lower Rathmines, turning left at the bridge to proceed along the Grand Canal. Smog cut visibility down to fifteen yards or so. Progress was careful but steady. It was now obvious to me that the contentment that coursed through my body was not prevalent among my fellow recruits.

'Sorry I joined.'

'I'm getting out.'

These snatches of conversation drifted to my ears above the steady noise of the engine. It wasn't the sort of camaraderie talk I'd expected from a bunch of brothers in arms. Indeed, what was to follow was a real shock. The lorry came to a halt at a set of traffic lights.

'I'm off,' Jefferson shouted. 'I've had enough. Fuck the army.' He then skipped over the tail end of the lorry with the agility of a mountain goat and was last seen making the best of his way through the foggy gloom. When I'd recovered from this initial shock, I shouted after his fast disappearing figure that he owed me half a quid. A resounding amplification, referring clearly to my hangers, was the derisive reply before he was swallowed up in the fog. The lorry gave a jolt and was just into second gear when surprise number two launched itself over the tailboard.

'Screw the Curragh!' were his parting words of comfort, as he dodged another vehicle bringing up the rear. The load was getting lighter. What was happening? I couldn't understand this alarming twist of events. They could be soldiers, by just sitting tight, and here they were lamming it, not having served a day, going on the run. Why go to the trouble of all the fuss and bother? The mind boggled. We continued down the canal; the remarks of discontent developed into a wail that would do justice to a gathering of nuns at a whores' convention. Why oh why didn't that damn corporal sit at his post which was back here in the rear of the truck? That would have halted their gallop for sure.

By the time we reached the next set of lights, which again happened to be red, another three had decided to abscond, easing themselves gently into the road to be swallowed up in the darkness. Goose pimples stood out on my exposed parts like buttercups. I didn't join in the general hullabaloo of the conversation, it was none of my business, but my heart was dropping, like the mercury in a barometer before a hurricane. If only the lorry would keep moving. At this rate there would be a gale of wind blowing through the wagon before the cursed conveyance reached the Curragh. The implications of these rash actions was playing havoc with my youthful feelings. Was I acting in some farce or comedy? Why didn't I wait 'til Tuesday? I admonished myself. I didn't have to enlist that Monday. These thoughts and many, many more were wheeled in a jumble of disorientated doubts which besieged my brain. The lorry was moving again. Those of us left would surely be shot, that thought crossed my mind too. A voice spoke from the canvas interior.

'Next stop I'm off.'

'Me too,' said another.

'I'm almost home, when we reach Inchicore.'

'Merciful God, stop them,' I groaned, changing my position to sit directly behind the cab. It was a little warmer there, and further from the tailboard. What I'd give for a smoke. I stuffed my hands into opposite sleeves of my coat and gradually inched as far as I could into the corner as if trying to escape from this horrible nightmare that was unfolding before my very eyes.

Sure enough, the lorry stopped again. By now I was past caring whether it was traffic lights or not. Resolve and resignation had taken over from apathy and mass desertion. At this rate it was surprising there was a soldier left in the army. If we ever had to do battle I reasoned, the first obstacle to surmount would be how to keep rookies in the open back of a truck. Two more 'elopers' escaped with a vault over the tailboard, I could hear their feet crunch on the road as they landed and their hasty retreat at the double.

'Oh well,' said one of the other two remaining. 'Only the three musketeers left, unless you decide to take the jump.' He spoke in my direction.

'No,' I said gloomily. 'It isn't for me, I'm staying put. I don't suppose you've got a smoke?' I continued.

'Sorry.'

I sighed.

'Anyway, I'm Harry,' he said.

'Jim,' I replied.

'Bernard,' coughed the other guy. 'And I don't smoke.'

'Holy cow! You don't smoke?' Harry almost choked.

'Well I used to,' Bernard offered. 'But I gave them up in prison.'

'In prison!' Harry almost exploded.

'Yeh, Mountjoy,' Bernard mumbled. 'Six months for grievous.

'Holy cow!' said Harry.

Silence reigned for ten minutes or so. We were all lost in our own thoughts.

'Wouldn't like to be in corporal's boots, would you?' Harry began.

'He'll certainly have a bit of explaining to do,' Bernard agreed. 'Probably lose his stripes if the truth were known.'

'Holy cow!' Harry gasped.

The lorry rushed on through the night. Harry gave a running commentary as we passed various landmarks. The fog and smog was now behind us, as we left the city limits and took to the country. The driver increased his speed to make up for lost time, no doubt with a pint in view when we reached our destination. As for the corporal, he would most definitely need a jar or two.

'This is Naas,' Harry drawled as the village high street receded in a bellow of exhaust fumes. 'Won't be long now, Newbridge next and we're almost there.'

Finally the lorry slowed to a halt. I heard the door of the driver's cab open. Hob nailed boots sounded on the gravel, the corporal sauntered back for what I would imagine to be the shock of his life. He gave the side of the wagon a resounding thump, shouting out 'You lot, let's have you, move yourselves!'

We did — all three of us.

The lorry had halted outside what would be our new home, McDonagh Barracks. We lined up, the corporal busied himself with the enlisted forms, ten of them. His eyes wandered from the forms to us three, then to the open back lorry. Back to the forms, then back to us again. A puzzled look crossed his face and he actually walked over to the wagon and peered inside. Lifting his cap, he scratched his head, looked at the forms again, had another blimp into the lorry and slowly walked back to where we stood to attention looking straight ahead and very unamused.

'Where's the fucking rest?' he said with disbelief.

I'd already heard it said that silence was golden and no better time than the present to put it to the test. I fervently hoped that Holy Cow would continue to chew the cud. His dialogue for the last thirty miles had been continuous and informative, why stop now? Much to my eternal relief he coughed politely and said, 'They deserted sir.'

'They deserted!' the corporal exclaimed. 'Did you hear that, Mick?' he shouted to the driver who, by now, had emerged from behind the wheel, obviously hearing the commotion.

'Seven of the bleeders have taken a fast "pony". Skedaddled! Now listen Mick,' the corporal spoke with urgency. 'The fog, don't forget the fog, it's my only chance. My bleeding stripes will sprout wings. It was foggy all of the way. Right, you got that" And I was in the cab helping with the navigation. Jaysus wept! Don't forget, I'll end up in the glasshouse.'

'Why didn't one of these bastards give us the word?' snapped Mick, looking at the three of us with obvious malice.

Holy Cow was just about to come to the rescue and say something when an Officer appeared. The corporal and the driver sprang to attention. As did we three.

'You've arrived corporal?' the Officer said, giving us new arrivals a satisfied smile. 'At ease,' he said.

'Could I have a word with you sir?' The corporal spoke hurriedly.

'Yes certainly. Something amiss?'

'I'll explain sir,' he exclaimed, leading the way out of earshot.

We stood where we were, I could just about hear the tone of voices rising up and down. A good five minutes elapsed before they returned to our presence. The enlistment forms were now in the hands of the Officer, who appeared very calm and collected; the immediate crisis seemed to have passed.

'Well lads,' the Officer said. 'It's now a question of who *is* present, and who isn't. From the left, your names.'

'Murtagh, Harold.'

'Purdy, James.'

'Price, Bernard,' came the third and final recruit.

The Officer sorted out the appropriate forms, keeping seven. He handed the other three to the corporal. 'Get these men settled in,' he ordered.

The corporal now seemed more cheerful. It would appear as if he was off the hook. The Officer went on to welcome us to the camp before bidding us good night.

'Attention!' the corporal barked. We sprang to attention.

'Right wheel, by the left, quick march.' Our destination was the Quarter Master's Store. There we stripped off and put our civvies in a canvas bag, provided. We were told it would be duly labelled and stored for our demob.

The big surprise was the size of my head. After trying on several caps the QM handed me a size seven and a half — the biggest in stock — it was the only one that fitted. We slipped into our fatigues and carried the rest of our kit to the billet. I was thrilled.

The billet was large and roomy. The beds were wooden boards sitting on trestles. A mattress, rather thin but ample, was spread out over the boards. The beds were about three feet apart. A turf fire burned homely in a large grate at the far end of the billet. On each side stood a line of rifles — Lee Enfield 303's. A chain running through the trigger guard then on to a padlock secured them to the wall. Grey blankets, two sheets and a pillow, a large box at the foot of the bed was for one's personal kit.

The billet was filled with new recruits who had arrived from other counties. We sat up 'til lights-out smoking and yarning; not all the recruits were devoid of funds.

A porch way or landing divided the billets where one washed and shaved in cold water. I was spared the discomfort of shaving. There just wasn't any growth of significance as yet on my face. The lavatories were situated slap in the middle of the square. This proved to be a bit of a hassle, especially for the soldiers who liked a jar, and most of them did imbibe. At my age I obviously didn't drink, but in uniform who could refuse to serve me? However, I didn't put it to the test. I'd no desire to drink then.

When it was raining it was infuriating having to cross the square to visit the bog. Each soldier had to don greatcoat, boots and cap. Diarrhoea was a complaint which sapped your strength in more ways than one. I, in my youthful innocence, slept soundly through most of these discomforts which inflicted many, but I heard the rumblings and complaints the following morning.

This first night I slept so well I didn't hear Reveille, and to my chagrin I was tipped out of my bed by a corporal. There were loud wails of laughter and remarks from the other occupants, some of whom had already made up their beds. The sheets had a blue line running through the middle, and had to be folded in a fine crease with the blue line peeping through — likewise the folding of the blanket.

Each soldier took it in turn to be room orderly, which was a chore liked by all. It really meant tidying the fire grate, keeping the fire burning and sweeping the floor. The billets were inspected every morning. Once the inspection had taken place, the rest of the morning was spent smoking and yarning with other room orderlies.

I somehow managed to stumble down the stone stairs on time with the rest. That first morning we were lined up in three rows and quickly shown the rudiments of 'square bashing'. It was seven o'clock. Soon the cold of the day gave way to a warm glow, as the blood coursed through the veins. An hour's marching to and fro across the wide expanse of tarmac invigorated the body and set a hearty appetite for breakfast which was at eight o'clock.

That first day, wearing the clodhoppers (or boots) made my young legs ache. The hunger too was gnawing at my stomach and the call for breakfast was more than welcome. A large sea of brown filed into the Mess — we were all in our fatigues. The Mess was similar to the one at Portobello Barracks — wooden forms with wooden tables to match. The breakfast was to me an excellent meal. The usual quarter of loaf and knob of butter, with black pudding and bacon and a pint mug of tea. When the meal was finished I really felt I'd had a decent fulfilling breakfast.

Back to the square at nine for Work Parade. The real training wouldn't take place for a couple of weeks. We were separated into sections of eight and marched off to do various tasks. The section I found myself in was detailed to a large compound filled with turf and surrounded by a huge wire fence. A lorry was standing by the mound of turf, waiting to be loaded. Eight of us got to work with relish. When we'd finished, it trundled off to the Officers' quarters, where another section would be waiting to unload it. This meant we had a breather in between loads.

As yet, no one had passed any remarks as to my age or youthful looks. It seemed as if I was accepted. Needless to say, this delighted me. The days were marred only by my penury. If only I'd had a few shillings my happiness would have been complete. Dinner was not as agreeable as breakfast. The potatoes were steamed and tasted accordingly. Still, who was I to complain? My plate was cleared in double quick time. Semolina was on offer for afters, with a blob of jam in the middle. It tasted delicious.

Our day ended at four in the afternoon. Afterwards we could shake down our beds or simply get into uniform and hit the town. A mouth organ player in any billet was an added bonus. A Wexford 'walla' was our source of entertainment. He played with a certain haunting tempo which lingers in my memory to this day.

Supper was served Mondays and Tuesdays only. Wednesday was pay day. The pay was issued at twelve o'clock. Wednesday was also sports half day. It was compulsory to attend whichever function our superiors had decided was best for our 'enjoyment', whether it be a hurling match or a soccer match. Indeed, even horse racing at the Curragh was deemed to be recreation. You fell in after dinner, and were duly marched with pomp and ceremony to the chosen venue, then dismissed. The older sweats would make for the nearest 'boozer', others would find their way back to camp where card schools would be in session, along with games of pitch and toss. This latter game was frowned on by the authorities. Blankets would be spread out on the floorboards to cushion the sound of the falling coins. Often these gatherings ended with tempers flaring and fists flying, as some rookie or other would find himself accused of cheating. I steered clear of these gatherings. Cheating was rife: some of the soldiers were experienced in dealing good hands of poker to unsuspecting greenhorns, always of course, with a better hand of cards for themselves, and in instances like that, one had to back-up any discovery with equally good fistycuffs. Some of the fights were gems to watch, others were very ugly and violent.

There were seven barrack blocks in all. Each was named after an Irish patriot who fell in the fight for independence. 'Connolly, 'Clark' and 'Kent' come to mind. Prior to the treaty it was a base for British Troops. The Curragh Plains, which stretch for miles, were surely a haven for the training of horse cavalry. Some years later, during a visit to Turkey (actually Hydarpasha, which is just across the Bosphorus from Istanbul) I came across an old Christian cemetery, the custodian being a Frenchman. On examining the faded headstones, I was surprised to see one in memory of a follower of the Curragh camp, who had died as a result of wounds in the Crimea. The graveyard was occupied by a pack of wild dogs who had made it their home. Needless to say, I didn't dilly dally, assuming, and reasonably so, that some of the dogs would be rabid.

A lot of the old British army words survived. Words brought back from India were in frequent use at the Curragh. 'Gilty', meaning smart. 'Gilty wallah', smart man; 'Buckshee', or 'bakshes' meaning free or gratis, and of course, 'char', the well-known name for tea.

I discovered the camp pawn broker. Being without money was the only thing that really bugged me. Forever smoking other soldiers' cigarettes was against the grain. The pawn broker was, in fact, another private — a three star private; the star system being worth an extra sixpence per day for each star awarded. After three, which was the maximum, one could go on to be a corporal — the position of lance-corporal and lance-sergeant being non-existent in the Free State. One shilling and sixpence per day or ten shillings and sixpence per week was worth chasing. The corporal's position was taboo and unpopular and it appeared that most were happy to stick to the three stars and call it a day. His 'Highness' the pawn broker was one of those privates. His head was well screwed on as the saying goes. You could pawn spare kit, such as socks and field dressing, even one's 'housewife' which consisted of a packet of needles and thread, or any bit of equipment which made up your soldier's kit. To pledge was easy, but the day of reckoning was the first Saturday of each month, this being the day of the CO's inspection. Lockers had to be left open, each soldier stood by his bed and one's kit was checked thoroughly. Any missing item had to be paid for in full. The last week of each month was a busy and profitable one for the pawn broker, as whole companies rushed to redeem their kit.

Sundays were traditionally a day of rest. Every other Sunday we paraded before breakfast to attend Mass and receive Holy Communion, assuming, of course, one had made a Holy Confession the previous day, and received absolution. On alternative Sundays we held Mass Parade after breakfast and marched off to chapel, accompanied by a band. These parades were compulsory for all Catholics. Protestants, who numbered three in our company, normally paraded before falling out, with orders to report to the Mess halls for duty. This, in my eyes, was better than the compulsory Mass parade which we had to attend week after week. On reaching the chapel the various units were dismissed which meant that you didn't actually have to attend the service or enter the church. Small knots of men used to congregate outside smoking and gossiping until Mass ended, then take their place in the line-up for the march back to the barracks.

It was an uphill slog all the way back to McDonagh and my young legs had to work overtime to keep in step with the culshie's goose-step. To say I felt crucified on such days, would be an accurate estimate of my feelings.

After being paid Wednesdays, most of the troops would be counting the pennies by the Sabbath. A very Protestant lady owned one of the two cinemas to be found in the garrison village. One was aptly named 'The Curragh' and the other one was known as 'Ma Sands'. Ma Sands had a service each Sunday evening, where the Gospel According to Saint Luke was suitably swallowed with the help of tea and cakes; this after exercising the vocal chords in a hymn or two. The tea and cakes was not the main attraction, however. Ma Sands used to part with two halfcrowns to would-be Protestants, and if Sunday morning saw the stream of Catholics heading for Mass, Sunday evening was even more spectacular, with as many Catholics moving towards Ma Sand's to line their pockets with the five bob on offer. So, needless to say private Jim Purdy joined the line of soldiers heading for the promised land and the joys therein. Considering only three Protestants fell out on Mass parade in the morning, the number by the evening had swelled dramatically. The 'soul' it seemed could be bought for a dollar. This money generously given and greedily accepted was sufficient to keep the billet in smokes until pay day.

Following the two weeks moving turf it was time to prepare for sterner stuff. The training tempo gained momentum, but first another more elaborate medical at the Curragh Military Hospital, a very large establishment. Chest X-rays came first and mine were clear of all ailments. The other tests for foreign bodies similarly proved negative.

An annexe to the main hospital housed an isolation unit where words such as 'clap' and 'dose' were whispered in awe. Back in those far off days I was unaware of such things as gonorrhoea and syphilis. Not wanting to show my ignorance, I nodded at the right time and gasped accordingly on hearing the whispered — 'Paddy has it.' I would stare at the isolation unit a great deal and watch the smoke curling skyward from Woodbine funnels that dominated the wooden huts which were used as wards. What was a dose? I wished I knew. With me Ma, a dose was always a dose of medicine but here there was something sinister lurking in the shacks behind the wire fence. What on earth was it? What fiendish germs waited to gobble you up? How in hell did the inflicted become infected? All these and many more questions were puzzles which would solve themselves with the passage of time. However, at that age I was impatient with a fervent longing to know. I tried various rouses to gain enlightenment. Lying on my bed at night I would broach the subject: 'How many do you reckon are in isolation with the clap?; 'After you get a dose, how long will you be in hospital?'; 'Can the disease kill?'

One night, the eagerly sought answer came. A soldier, busy boning the toe of his boots with a toothbrush handle, said 'I reckon it's the same bitch that gives it to the whole garrison. After all, there aren't many girls that will drop their drawers to the first man that happens along.'

He made this statement as if he were addressing the whole billet. I put my hands behind my head and lay back on my pillow to ponder this shocking revelation. A barrack room lawyer ceased polishing his buttons and joined in the conversation.

'The germ of syphilis comes from the camel,' he stated with the air of a man who knew what he was talking about.

'No wonder they have the hump,' said another with a chuckle.

'Well it's true if you want to pass the buck back, it will stop squarely at the camel's arse.'

'What you're saying then, in reality, is someone, somewhere screwed a camel,' said the latter, a Cork man called McGee. 'You'll tell me next,' he continued, 'it was a regiment from the Curragh.'

'No,' said the former seriously, 'in all probability it was an Arab, and why not. There are rumours that the poor innocent sheep of the Curragh Plains have been subjected to indecent acts. It happened at Scapaflow during the War, why not the Curragh?'

'Where is Scapaflow?' I asked.

'Doesn't know where Scapaflow is! What school did you attend! Ignorant little bugger. North Scotland,' said McGee, looking in my direction. 'Anyway,' he said, addressing the lawyer, 'was it a male or female camel or just camels in general?'

'Would it make any difference what sex it was? They dress the same don't they?'

'A big or little difference to the camel,' replied McGee, 'and that's important.'

'The sheep outside my window are looking lovelier by the minute,' said the lawyer.

'You've put me off lamb for life,' McGee said, disgusted.

'Just close your eyes and creep up behind one,' said the lawyer.

'The army doesn't supply wellington boots,' McGee replied.

'More's the pity,' the lawyer sighed.

'Where do the wellington boots come in?' I queried, looking somewhat puzzled.

'That's an idiot if there ever was one,' the lawyer purred.

'Nothing between the ears. Prairie brains,' agreed McGee.

'Miles apart,' said the other in agreement.

I was going against my better judgement asking questions. It was time I clamped up and kept my great trap shut. Be like the three wise monkeys — I told myself — hear, see and say nothing.

'What's the army coming to? What age are you Purdy? And don't insult my intelligence by telling me you're eighteen,' he warned good humouredly.

'No, I'm not eighteen,' I replied. 'I'm twenty-one.'

'Twenty-one? Did you hear that, McGee? Lies like a pig in shit. Spins more yarn than a Lancashire cotton mill. Weaves a web of lies around himself. If he's twenty-one, then my mother's a Godfather to Churchill.'

'Aye, and my Ma gets a living stuffing pillows from hair taken from a banshee's fanny. McGee laughed out loud. 'What do you say to that, you little Dublin chancer?'

'Nothing,' I said, 'nothing at all.'

McGee spat on the toe of his boot for the umpteenth time. The vigorous friction of the toothbrush handle was taking effect. The toe of the boot was red and glossy. Ox Blood polish seemed to be the favourite. I quickly got undressed and crept between the sheets.

'Bet you miss your Ma's goodnight kiss,' the lawyer teased, still polishing the brass buttons on his jacket.

'Ah, leave the poor creature alone,' McGee cried. 'Homesick to be sure. I wouldn't be surprised to see his Ma here tomorrow with his pram to fetch him home.' I didn't hear much more as I slipped from drowsiness to contented sleep.

As the weeks wore on I became more confident. I was in the money too, picking up my twenty-seven shillings each Wednesday and sending ten shillings every week home to Ma, knowing well she would be glad of it. Brasso, cigarettes, polish and tooth-paste — items of each were purchased from the canteen enough to suffice for the coming week. My remaining teeth were being cleaned for the first time in their life. My gums bled freely, they were not used to such meticulous attention. I persisted but all to no avail, for by the age of thirty, every tooth in my head had been exchanged for dentures.

The eighteen inch bayonet was then the standard issue, surplus stock from the First war. Clipping it into the bayonet boss one morning I found myself charging across the Curragh Plains. The objective was a straw dummy which was straddled from a cross-bar. Another lay on the ground, no doubt mortally wounded. Thrust in, twist, pull out. Wheel to the left at the double and back to the starting point where the whole process was repeated.

By lunch time I'd have gladly changed places with the dummy, I was so exhausted. The whistle went, play was over 'til after dinner. I staggered back to the billet, I just couldn't face the dinner and opted instead for the canteen. I had a little money to spare and treated myself to a pint of milk and a jam doughnut. The milk was cold and tasted delicious, it certainly put a bit of pep back into my aching limbs. After dinner the straw dummy was declared redundant, much to my relief, in its place was a lesson on the hand-grenade type miles bomb, weight, one and a half pounds, with a seven second fuse. We stripped it and put it back together again before finally throwing it at a circle of sand-bags. A simulated machine gun post. The exercise was not so strenuous as the straw dummy and I was glad of the respite it afforded. Looking back I don't think I'd have lasted the day if the bayonet instruction lesson had continued throughout the afternoon.

By tea time I was feeling my old self and devouring the offering of eggs and beans that was on the menu. Sometime prior to all this active training I was shown a list of army careers and invited to choose one. I, at that time, said my preference was the infantry as opposed to artillery or cavalry. Why I chose the infantry, I don't know. Perhaps I was brain-washed by the current spate of war films. The rifles which were allocated to us were actually useless as weapons. They were issued only to raw recruits for drill. When we finally got around to doing some shooting we were issued with other rifles for our stint at the range. The Lee Enfield '303' fires with a snapping, whipping crack. The recoil, or kick as it was widely known, did, if not properly held, give one an almighty jolt. The proper way to hold a rifle is to tuck the butt firmly into your shoulder, keeping the tip of the foresight in the 'V' of the rear sight, and squeeze the trigger, and I mean squeeze, not pull — pulling the trigger could, and sometimes did, result in a dislocated shoulder. My performance on the range was not spectacular, in fact, not even average, but it was my first visit and I was hopeful of showing some improvement. There was certainly scope for it.

That evening after firing at ranges from one to three hundred yards, plus a silhouette target, my shoulder was black and blue. Bruises I was proud to have for no particular reason. The first and last punishment I endured was on a Saturday morning; a day of much activity. It was the day of the month when all things had to be cleaner than clean for the CO's inspection. The day when your brass buttons shine 'til they don't look like brass at all. Boots polished to the outer limits of cleanliness — insteps included; the eyelets of the boots were polished too. Cap badges glittered beyond the gleam of perfection, the buckles of the webbing were not forgotten either in the mad haste of one company to outshine another.

Unknown to the rest of the billet a large and awkward culshie got fell-in with boots that just weren't up to the standard. The oil seeping from the brown leather had spread across the surface until the white on the dark tan resembled spats. This was one of the drawbacks of the standard issue. But they could be camouflaged for a half hour or so, at least until the inspection was over. This idiot just hadn't bothered, or the importance of the occasion just wasn't brought home to his hay-harvesting head. It was the only pause the CO made on his otherwise slow and deliberate walk along the routes of stiffed-back ranks. His cane pointed to the offending footwear and one could see the sergeant's face bulge, and could detect the build-up of invective that would burst forth like a breached dam on the CO's departure. The inspection finished with all rookies standing by their beds, lockers had been examined for missing kit but all had been redeemed from the camp's pawnbroker.

When the CO departed having satisfied himself that we were still self-sufficient soldiers, an uneasy calm descended. Normally we would be finished for the remainder of the day: alas, not many minutes passed before the irate sergeant surged through the door. The explosion of invective spilled over us like diarrhoea. The final affront arose when he casually ordered the whole billet to change into fatigues and line up on the square. The order was carried out with mounting apprehension and threats of physical violence launched in hayhead's direction. He, in turn, was looking squeamish and uncomfortable.

We left the billet in dribs and drabs but in less than five minutes we had assembled in our brown fatigues. The sergeant looked as if his mother-in-law had brought her sister along for a lengthy stay. We marched off three abreast from the barracks, heading for the sprawling Curragh Plains. Most of us by then had guessed our fate. After a quarter of a mile we were ordered to double up, a groan rising into the air from the ranks. The sergeant standing perfectly still let us trundle off across the Curragh and just before we doubled out of earshot the screech of 'left wheel' echoed. Running now obliquely, with the sergeant's still form, 'left wheel' was again ordered and we were trotting back to our starting point and so the punishment continued, running around in circles.

Fortunately we didn't have full packs. I know for a fact I wouldn't have survived the gruelling doubling to and fro. My lack of years told on my stamina and I was soon showing signs of distress. Before long my shirt was wet and clinging to my back. I struggled on every turn and every shout of 'left wheel' became agonisingly painful. Gasps and groans of discomfort could be heard, boots full of feet somehow kept going, urged on by each other.

'Keep moving. Don't fall out, it'll only be worse.'

These words and others kept the ranks together. Time was a

blur, the ranks became bedraggled and began to spread out as each individual became a running, steaming ball of heat. I'd now reached the end of my tether, there was nothing left, I'd run out of fuel. With a final gasp of surrender I fell to my knees. The saliva gathered at my mouth and sweat burned my eyes, blurring my vision. I pulled my sleeve across my forehead. My throat was dry and parched. I could make out a pair of boots standing at angles, they were shining and gleaming red in contrast to the green of the grass. My name was being called.

'Purdy!' The unmistakable voice of our present tormentor. I couldn't answer, I was gasping in great lungs full of air.

'Purdy, are you all right?'

In short the answer was no, but I said nothing. The voice was more concerned now. Arms were lifting me to my wobbly feet. I noticed the other recruits had stopped, most with their arms bent on their knees, each fighting his own battle to regain some form of composure. The sergeant satisfied himself I'd live.

'Let's get fell-in,' he snapped. Soldiers were lifting themselves from various parts of the Plains, moving back into rank. I could feel my face go white. Christ! Don't faint, I admonished myself.

'Now we shall march back,' the sergeant bawled. 'Anyone out of step will find himself doubling up again — line up properly, shoulders back, quick march. Left, left, left, right, left.' And off we went back to the barracks. We reached the square, and with sighs of relief the Company was dismissed. Tired legs were dragged up concrete steps. Beds were quickly spread out, and boots removed with a clatter. The culshie was spared for the moment; all energy was spent. I being the first to succumb to the recruits' gruelling punishment was now feeling sheepish.

Dinner hour was fast approaching and I decided to go to the Mess — straight into the lion's mouth as it turned out. My thoughts of bed that Saturday afternoon were soon shattered. Half way through the pork and veg an officer entered the Mess accompanied by an NCO. This was nothing new. In fact, they always appeared at meal times, strolling between the tables, pausing here and there to inquire if there were any complaints, not that anyone would dare complain. Never once did a rookie rise to his feet to voice dissatisfaction, least of all me. However it wasn't my lucky day. The officer having done his rounds among the rows of tables, stopped at the table where I sat. His cane cracked down on the wooden top. Eating and conversation ceased abruptly.

'All at this table,' he ordered curtly, 'to report for duty at the cookhouse at two sharp.' With that he moved on and out of the Mess, leaving behind a complement of eight swearing soldiers. One denounced himself for not visiting the canteen while another announced knowingly that we were detailed for spud bashing, that's exactly what the order turned out to be. All eight of us arrived at the cook-house promptly at two. The cook didn't beat about the bush. Pointing to a heap of potatoes he said, 'That lot there to be peeled.'

Armed with knives we set about our task. It seemed to me to be a formidable job of work. There were eight one-hundred-weight sacks. 'One sack to each,' someone suggested.

I sat on an upturned bucket and began to peel. It didn't take as long as I'd expected. Within an hour we were putting the spuds in soak and generally tidying up the peelings into large drums to be collected later for 'swill' by a local farmer.

The following week, while doing some square bashing, I noticed an officer standing by the armoury, his eyes never left me as he spoke to an NCO by his side. We marched to the far side of the square and did an about turn and marched smartly back: each time his eyes followed me. I'd reached a state of mind where all the hurdles had been cleared and no more obstacles remained. I was acting like a soldier, training like a soldier, and generally I was accepted as a fellow soldier by my fellow recruits. Yet this officer's consistent interest in me made me feel uneasy. I calmed my fears telling myself it was my imagination. The company came to a halt and a lesson in arms drill was next on the agenda. I was on the extreme left of the rank as we sloped, presented and ordered arms. The arms lesson lasted half an hour. The officer was still there, occasionally turning his head to address the NCO and immediately his head was swivelling back in my direction. There was something wrong, something amiss, but what?

'Fall out for a smoke,' came the order signalling the end of the lesson in arms drill. I made a move to get amongst the ranks as they split up for their smoke. Out of sight, out of mind, I decided. What happened next was completely unexpected. The NCO who was, in fact, a sergeant left the Officer's side and approached the corporal who had been putting us through our paces. Whispered words passed hurriedly between them. I noticed the corporal glancing at me and nodding. I dragged deeply on my smoke. What now? I mumbled a silent prayer to The Almighty. Surely nothing could go wrong now, not after all I'd been through. Christ in his infinite wisdom surely would have mercy?

'Purdy.' The word was cold and impersonal.

'Sir,' I said, simply standing to attention.

'You're to report to the CO.'

'Me, sir? Why, sir?' I gulped.

'Don't ask questions, Purdy, just do as you're told. Haven't you learnt that much yet?'

'Yes, sir. Sorry, sir.'

'Finish your smoke first. No need to break into a gallop.'

'Thank you, sir.' I gulped again.

Leaning against the wall my mind raced back over the previous days. I hadn't misbehaved. I couldn't recall any reason for this instant call to the CO's presence. This could only mean one thing, but surely not? I tried to console my rising fears. Commonsense told me what to expect. The time to fall in again arrived and I immediately made my way to the CO's office, my heart sinking with every step. The CO smiled, it was a nice friendly smile.

'Name, rank and number?' These I reeled off and waited for the next question.

'What age are you, Purdy?' So the dreaded moment had arrived along with the taboo subject.

'Eighteen sir,' I heard myself say.

'And your date of birth?'

'Twenty fifth of March, Nineteen thirty sir.'

'Very well Purdy, now tell me your real age.'

'Eighteen sir,' eyes looking straight ahead. The officer still smiled and spoke in kindly tones. He never once raised his voice in argument. I for my part never once wavered in my determination to convince him.

Finally he said, 'We know your real age, Purdy. You are a mere fourteen years old, so why not admit it?' I remained adamant. Two months had passed since I'd joined up. I was a soldier and wanted to remain a soldier. 'Very well, Purdy.' His sigh was audible, the interrogation was at an end.

I made an about turn and quickly marched out of the office. Back in the billet I confided in the room orderly. He listened in sympathy and we shared a cigarette. 'What next?' I asked despairingly.

'You'll be drummed out,' he answered casually. 'Anyway, they check everyone's age thoroughly. You didn't expect to get away with it did you?'

I lay in bed that night pondering my predicament. Hoping against hope that when I awoke it would be just a bad dream. Alas, it was not to be. The very next day I was taken off the now rigorous training schedule. I was detailed to report to the Mess for duty, clearing away plates, washing dishes, and making large urns of tea.

The days dwindled by. My comrades' conversation centred on the machine gun, the bren gun and the other weapons an infantry soldier was trained to use. I continued to join in the apparent jocularity of the company as they were moulded into shape.

All the tasks, petty ones at that, were put my way. My pay was cut by half. 'The balance will be held until your demob,' I was told. 'You are to be discharged.'

# Chapter 12

The end had come to a very satisfying period of my life. Two weeks were to elapse before I finally walked out through the gates for the last time. During these last weeks I had to return my kit; my paltry belongings were handed back. No more spit and polish for me, the days became long and boring with nothing to do. I felt very self-conscious, hanging about the billet in my civvies. My short-term pals were kindness itself, I was never short of a cigarette or a treat to the pictures. Some tried to cheer me up with remarks like, 'I wish I was getting my ticket', 'Christ, I've signed up for three years', or 'You have it made, Purdy.'

Well, no one knew the real truth. I did, and I certainly didn't have it made. What would the outside world hold for me now? I felt empty. The secure wall I'd built up around myself was now blitzed, in bits, shattered. The goodbyes were not painful, there weren't any. I didn't know the day or hour of my departure.

When I did get to know, it was a mere five minutes' notice. My comrades were all out on the range. It was a Friday morning, just before eleven o'clock. I was ordered to take my belongings to the headquarters of the big chief himself. (What belongings? I hadn't any.) He was the camp commandant; a man I'd never set eyes on. He was large and frightening. I stood there like a chimpanzee gazing at King Kong. He glanced at me with the contempt I deserved, the look I understood only too well. Any feelings of sorrow I'd nourished for myself soon vanished under a barrage of abuse. It generated an impulse to retaliate. I felt my short temper flare. However, I was still officially in the army and had often seen the prison called the glasshouse and had heard many a tale of woe, and the degradation that occurred behind the grey walls of that establishment.

'Well, what do you think this is?' the Commandant roared, 'the fucking boy scouts?'

'No sir,' I squirmed at this remark.

'Sign here,' he ordered. 'And get out of my sight before I do something I might regret. That's your travelling warrant' (my ticket), he said, throwing a piece of paper on the desk. 'I've a good mind to make you walk the twenty-seven miles to Dublin. Go on, get moving before I change my mind.'

I closed the door hurriedly behind me. The bus stop was only a short walk from the camp. It all happened so quickly. Feeling dazed, I reached the stop only to find the bus had just departed for Dublin. Only an hour to wait for the next one. Well, I had a packet of smokes and seven shillings, that was a damn sight more than I had on arrival.

I discovered some months later that it was my Ma who informed the authorities of my age. I now became a corner boy after my stint in the army, the only jobs available would be the usual messenger-boy type. The void left after being a Freestater could not be filled by pedalling a bike.

My next job was the result of my father's efforts. He managed to get me an apprenticeship in the Liffey Dock Yard. I was now sixteen years old. My wages for the first year were to be nine shillings and ninepence per week, rising to nineteen shillings and ninepence on the commencement of the second year. A whole one pound rise in the third year, accumulating to four pounds seven shillings and sixpence on my fifth and last year. I was to remain dutifully learning a trade until I was twenty-one years old. I was to follow the family tradition and become a shipwright. It was a good and reasonable trade to learn, especially in a small yard like the Liffey.

The odd schooner was still hauled up the slipway. The usual ships were cargo types being converted for cattle, horses and sheep to the UK or Belgium. What I didn't know or realise was that this honourable trade was dying a slow but natural death; the rot had already set in. Nevertheless I got stuck into the art of using an adze and other relevant tools. We, in those days, had orders for wooden 'main masts' and derricks, starting with a large 'four square' length of pitch or 'Oregon Pine'. We would set about it like a swarm of locusts, transforming the four square into eight, then sixteen to thirty-two. Of course, in the process, one would become very proficient in handling an adze. The circle would be completed with the main body of shipwrights wielding the jack plane. This was excellent work for keeping the circulation going during winter months.

On the cold mornings, and there were plenty of them, we would gather around the devil. It wasn't Satan as such, in fact it was a five gallon drum with a series of holes punched in the sides. Large holes about one inch in diameter at various angles for ventilation. This was our fire. There was always plenty of shavings and cut-offs lying about the shipwrights' shed, a giant source of fuel. The steam would rise visibly from our overalls or boiler suits, dampness that had accrued from the previous day's work. After jostling each other to edge nearer to the devil we'd be off to our designated jobs — invariably the dry stock or slipway or the shipwrights' shed.

In those bygone days the cattle, sheep and horse boats brought plenty of work to the yard, especially on their arrival for annual overhaul. Overtime was scarce but the odd occasion did arise. Overtime rates for the first year apprenticeship amounted to the staggering sum of one shilling per hour, still, every little helps, as the gnat said after pissing into The Liffey!

On the home front, things had changed slightly for the better. My eldest sister had married and moved from home. My eldest brother Jack was also married. The next down the line, Brian, was in the Free State Army, although by this time Ireland or Eire had been declared a Republic. Brian was stationed at Clancy Barracks, situated near the famous Phoenix Park, famous for its size, and walks. Lord Cavendish was to meet his death there at the hands of the Fenians before the turn of the century. Dublin's Zoo is there also. It had made quite a name for itself by successfully breeding lions in captivity. Another brother, Liam, had opted for the Irish Navy. In reality this was a fishery protection outfit and nothing more. Three Corvettes was the full strength of our Naval forces, bought second-hand from the British Admiralty. All three were re-christened and given Gaelic names, *The Clive*, *The Mave* and *The Moocha*, and a popular ditty went thus:

> The Clive, the Mave and the Moocha,
> The pride of the Irish Navy,
> They go to sea after breakfast,
> And then they sail home for their tea.

The Irish Naval Station is situated in County Cork, at Haulboline.

These four having fled the nest made our lot at home much easier. I was soon elevated from the floor to a double bed, which was shared with some younger brothers. Food too, had come off the ration. Although it was still fried bread for breakfast, there were sandwiches of cheese or brawn to take to work and stew or fried mince and mash for dinner. Of course, tea and a couple of cuts was there to be had at any time. I used to discuss my various jobs of work with my father. He never stinted and always gave me the benefit of his vast knowledge.

A small metal disc was issued at the Dockyard gate on one's arrival for work. The gateman handed these out when you called your number, mine was thirty-seven. Those failing to collect their number forfeited a day's pay. Five minutes late cost the late comer a quarter of an hour's pay, and ten minutes would result in a half hour going west. I arrived late one unforgettable morning, twenty minutes to be exact, and was promptly suspended for a whole week. This unexpected suspension was a particularly hard blow to accept. I needed the money more than ever. I was courting and after the Army I had taken a more distinct interest and pride in my appearance, although my wardrobe still consisted of only my working clothes and a change for Sundays.

Mass was for Sunday, as work was for Monday, necessary. Failing to attend Mass on Sundays and other days of Obligation was, in the eyes of the Catholic faith, 'committing a mortal sin' and the faith decreed that to die with a mortal sin on one's soul was to suffer hell fire and damnation. Needless to say, with that threat over your head, a special effort was made to attend Chapel, hence the crowds and throngs of people coming and going in the direction of the various churches on Sundays. There were plenty of churches, pubs and betting shops, each one seeking the few shillings that were in circulation.

To have 'sins on one's soul' meant going to Confession. One's 'soul' had to be cleansed and purged of sin. Absolution had to be received from the priest in attendance. A penance was given in the shape of prayers. These had to be recited at the altar before Holy Communion was received. One endeavoured to have Confession heard at least once a month. It was, and is, a psychological process culminating in taking the Holy Sacrament. This had to be undertaken the following morning before breakfast.

At the age of sixteen, I really hadn't given any serious thought to religion. It was just a groove one got into and continued by following the flock. The pennies and threepenny bits would be collected at the church door by wardens. The priest in his pulpit would remind the congregation that had gathered, that the church was in dire financial straits. One painfully obvious perception was the fact that the priests themselves always and without exception, seemed well fed and certainly well clothed and shod, and if they expired like the rest of their flock, it most certainly was not from malnutrition.

It was at this age that I would sever all connections with the Catholic Church, indeed, all Churches, and become and remain an atheist. It wasn't planned or plotted to any degree. It happened suddenly one Saturday evening. An evening which was normally a busy one for priests, as people rushed to prepare their souls for the Holy Sacrament.

The church was somewhat full when I entered. The seats were long highly polished pews, the movement in and out of the Confessional Box was slow, people seemed to be entering and leaving at a snail's pace. If a person was any length of time inside it was assumed he or she had committed something akin to murder. Sometimes the voice of the priest would rise as if shocked and heads would turn to gaze in awe at the 'box' and wait for the door to open, to get a glimpse of the person as he or she emerged.

Some priests were much quicker than others in dispensing absolution. The priests' names were displayed in bold black capitals on white cards above the Confessional Box. The box was built in three sections and lay against the flank wall of the church. The priest sat in the centre section and the would-be confessor entered a door on either side of him. A small sliding hatch would open and the priest would normally begin with 'Yes, my child'. The Confessional was in a state of complete darkness; some would say 'Thank God for that'. We began by ridding our souls of the lesser venial sins. To die in the Catholic Faith with only venial sins on your soul actually meant your soul went to purgatory, known as a place or state of rest where some souls suffer for a time before going to Heaven. In fact, the state of purgatory existed long before the Catholics latched onto it. Purgatory is mentioned in the Old Jewish Faith.

As I hadn't committed any mortal sins, knowingly that is, it was reasonable to assume that I wouldn't be detained for any length of time either in the Confessional or for that matter in Purgatory. When eventually the door opened, signalling my turn to enter I did so, light-heartedly. However, the events that followed came as a shock, surprise, call it what you will. I began my confession in low tones, always bearing in mind the long line of other sinners perched just outside the door. It must be said that in the silence of the Chapel even the slightest cough could be heard the length and breadth of the building.

'Bless me, Father, for I have sinned, it is four weeks since my last confession' — and so on. I merrily continued purging my soul of the sins I'd accumulated during the previous month. The priest remained silent until I'd finished or thought I'd finished. I then waited patiently for my penance expecting no more than a couple of Hail Marys and a Glory Be or two thrown in for good measure. However, the priest had other ideas, which were to give me quite a jolt.

'How do you sleep, child?' he asked rather bluntly.

'How do you sleep, Father?' I mimicked, parrot fashion, as if hearing things.

'Yes, how do you sleep?' he insisted, this time with a hint of impatience in his voice.

'I sleep very well, Father,' I said, somewhat bemused.

'I don't mean that.' He hissed the words rather loudly.

'Well, what do you mean, Father?' I asked, more bewildered than ever.

'You lay on your back or your side, I dare say, like most people,' he prompted.

'Yes, Father,' I gulped, hoping at the same time he wasn't a brownie.

'Where do your hands be?' He continued with the cross-examination, 'under the bedclothes, or above the bedclothes?'

'It depends on the weather, Father,' I answered, still not aware, indeed, ignorant as to the point he was endeavouring to put over.

'Well, child, let's say they're beneath the bedclothes,' he grated, his voice rising a couple of octaves. The penny was at last beginning to drop. My mouth suddenly felt dry.

'Do you use your hands to manipulate your private parts?' he asked. A thought crossed my mind that it would be awkward to use your feet. But by now I was feeling acutely embarrassed, and I simply answered 'Yes.'

'So you masturbate?' he roared. Jaysus, the whole congregation will know I'm a wanker. The thoughts made me groan inwardly as I nodded agreement. 'Why didn't you confess the fact?' he exploded.

'I didn't realise it was a sin, Father,' I replied miserably.

'You didn't know it was a sin?' he echoed. Christ, forget the congregation, all of Dublin knows by now!

'What school did you attend?' the priest continued.

'Crumlin Christian Brothers,' I whispered with a very strong desire to be somewhere else.

'What standard did you attain?' This information was quickly conveyed in a whisper.

A deep sense of shock had set in. The priest by now was

obviously in his element. 'My child, masturbating is the sin of Impurity, you will cease this filthy habit at once! Do I make myself clear?'

'Yes Father,' I said, never having heard it called masturbating before. As for the sin of Impurity, it too was another first. The agony of this little episode came to an end. My penance, needless to say, fitted the crime. It included several decades of the Rosary, the Stations of the Cross (this latter representing the stops Jesus made on his way to Mount Calvary) with Acts of Contrition thrown in for good measure. Those waiting outside the Confessional by now would have guessed I was 'Jack the Ripper'. I stumbled out very worried, and very angry. Many inquisitive eyes were upon me or was it my imagination. However, anger won the day. I took one last look at the Altar and walked out of the Chapel, never to return to it or the Catholic Faith again!

Masturbating in my view, is a natural biological process and does no harm whatsoever, whether it be of the male or female variety. There undoubtedly would be less rapists and sex offenders in jail today if they had paused to masturbate, thus relieving their urges and the tensions. I've been to many Chapels since to attend funeral services and weddings. But, having left the Catholic Church, a great burden was removed from my conscience. The burden of pretence and hypocrisy.

My apprenticeship passed agonisingly slow. Most of my weekends I spent sea fishing. There was an abundance of fish to be caught in and around the Dublin coastline. Saturday afternoons were spent gathering rag worm for the Sunday sport. With such large and varied fish to be caught, why were people hungry? A hand line and hook thrown from a pier-head would result in catches sufficient to fill one's belly for days. Pollock, pouting, plaice and whiting were in plentiful supply, not to mention the ever-present tope or dog-fish which makes an excellent meal when the skin is removed and is mostly sold as rock salmon in local fish and chip shops. A typical day's sea angling for me would commence at eight in the morning and finish about midnight. I never returned empty handed. There was always fresh fish on the plate for Monday's dinner. Hunger was at bay.

A girl entered my life at this time and a courtship blossomed. I couldn't afford to wine and dine her to any great extent. The cinema once a week was the best we could do. A kiss and a cuddle on taking her home was one's reward — to go further was unthinkable. To become pregnant out of wedlock was something of a national disgrace. There were, of course, girls who were utterly determined to get a husband and who knew more of the facts of life than their young and inexperienced male counterparts. When pregnancy was diagnosed, a hurried wedding would be arranged, often resulting in the youngsters continuing to live with their parents, until the young man was old enough and able enough to fend for his wife and family. The Dublin girls were far more advanced in sexual education than Dublin's young men. As for the rest of Ireland — well, I'm not qualified to answer for the other counties. One thing for sure, marriage for a young Dublin girl was the ultimate prize. It didn't really matter if they were widowed within a week or separated either, they had been married, that was their goal. What they earned they spent on clothes and cosmetics to show themselves off to the best advantage. The dance halls were a must for all eligible girls. Fridays and Saturdays were the 'hunting' days. To take a girl courting really meant 'running the gauntlet' — of the mother. If you admitted to taking a jar or two, you were immediately under suspicion but if you abstained and were learning a trade, then the handcuffs were out and you were on the wanted list. The best cups would appear from the china cabinet, a clean lace trimmed tablecloth appeared on the table, the bait was set.

Through this period, I struggled with my paltry earnings and shoddy clothes to keep up appearances. By my eighteenth birthday, I realised I'd reached the legal age to join the army, but the desire to be a soldier had faded. I was happy enough slogging away in the dockyard and looking forward to receiving my credentials, having now a strong desire to go to sea. A ship's carpenter was a reasonable position and there was a big wide world out there which had been discovered by others, but was yet to be explored by me. This then was the force that drove me on to finish my apprenticeship of five years and, hopefully, make me an adequate shipwright. I'd seen other guys in the yard finish their time and depart on foreign ships. They returned months later with large sun-tanned smiles and pockets well lined with the necessary! Knowledgeable talk of ports and cities abroad added strength to my desire to weigh anchor an sail away from it all.

At the age of twenty-one, with two affairs behind me, I was still a virgin. I had about five months of my time to serve but at this stage of our apprenticeship we were employed doing journeyman's work. I decided to approach the management and ask for my indentures. They were unsympathetic to this reasonable request, in fact a very blunt 'No' was the short answer.

I decided to take matters into my own hands and formally gave a week's notice of my intention to terminate my employment. My parents spent most of this week castigating me for being hasty and foolish. Impulsive was a word frequently used. However, the decision had been taken, there would be no turning back. I had in the interim approached the relevant union branch. Their reaction was more favourable and flexible. Provided, of course, I left Ireland and sought work abroad they would provide me with a document stating I was a qualified shipwright. The emigration wheels were now in motion.

My last week at the dockyard was one of mounting excitement, a new sense of freedom prevailed. I was twenty-one with a trade tucked under my belt. I was leaving Ireland, like millions had done before me. I gathered around me the few tools I'd accrued over the years, nothing much, certainly not a full set — mostly castaways from other men who could afford to buy more sophisticated tools. Friday loomed, I couldn't wait. I remember the two girls in the factory chanting 'God send Friday' — well, of all the Fridays, this was the one I wanted and desired most. My fcw belongings were packed.

When Friday did arrive I handed in my disc for the last time. A milestone was passed. My elder brother Brian who was now demobbed from the Irish Army had married and made his home in a place called Shirley, on the outskirts of Birmingham. He had a spare room and I needed to earn some real money, to replenish my tools and my wardrobe. I left the dockyard that evening carrying my toolbox on my shoulder and made my way along the north wall of the Liffey. My destination was the left luggage office of the British and Irish Steam Packet Company. I reached the luggage office after changing shoulders several times, the box was heavy and awkward.

The attendant gave me a ticket. 'Another one for England?' he said.

'Yes,' I grinned, delight showing in every crevice.

'Don't believe all you hear about over there,' he snapped, jabbing his finger towards the mouth of the Liffey.

'Can't be any worse than here,' I countered.

'Can't it?' he retorted. 'Huh! You'll see soon enough! Don't you believe all that crap about the streets being paved with gold. Sweat and tears, that's what they're paved with, nothing else. I've two lads over yonder,' he continued. 'They can't wait to come home. As a matter of fact, they're coming home Christmas for good.'

'Where will they get a job here?' I ventured.

'Jaysus, you only have to look at the boat every night. Every eligible man is fucking off. And what about the poor girls? What's going to happen to them. No youngsters here to marry them. A right state of affairs if you ask me.'

The steamer was filled to capacity. Cattle below decks and humans above. The ship was soon underway, moving slowly down the river. I stood at the stern, looking back at the fading lights of the city with mixed feelings. Behind, I was leaving years of want and yet there was a pervading sense of sadness and loss. In my pocket was a single pound note with some odd change. I had no real regrets, I was off to make my fortune. What lay ahead was in the future. There was certainly no future in the wake of the m/v *Munster*.

The wind freshened as the ship sailed past the harbour mouth, the engines increased their revs. People began moving off the decks to seek the warmth of the interior. I could see my old place of employment. The gantry and cranes lying silent and awkward, in silhouette against the darkened sky.

Leaving the deck, I made my way to the ship's bar where a lot of noisy singing was in progress. Another couple of pounds would have been welcome at this stage, to brace myself with porter and join in the merriment. However, I rejected the impulse to spend any of the little money in my possession.

Once outside the breakwater, the movement of the ship became sluggish and it began to roll and pitch. When the sea got a little rougher, faces grew greener. The lusty singing tailed off to the odd insignificant burst as passengers curled up in every available seat and corner.

It was a ten hour crossing, and sleep came in short naps. It was about six in the morning when I finally heaved myself to my feet and made my way, gingerly, through strewn and prone bodies to the washroom. I needed to freshen up before we docked at Liverpool. I felt more elated now that the initial hurdle was cleared. The washroom smelled strongly of vomit. Sea-sickness had left its mark on most of the receptacles. I cleaned one thoroughly and set about shaving. Having satisfied myself that I looked presentable, I emerged on deck and there it was in the misty distance — England.

The salt air smarted my recently shaved face. I took a deep breath of early morning air. A good-to-be-alive feeling coursed through my veins. I stood there for several minutes taking it all in. The stiffness soon left my body, I felt like a new man embarking on a new life. A nice cup of tea and a sandwich was by now a must. I could afford to spend some of my loose change. The lone pound note was sacred and not to be touched. The ship had slowed down considerably. Our destination was clearly in sight. Birkenhead first, to land the cattle; animals before humans. Hundreds of head of cattle poured from the ship's side, pushing and sliding down the gang planks to be slaughtered. The smell from the 'tween decks was nauseating, it certainly didn't encourage passengers to linger in the vicinity. Once the last of these unfortunate beasts had been prodded ashore, the ship moved across the Mersey to disembark hoards of hopeful immigrants.

Soon I sat perched on a bus bound for Lime Street Station, there to hump my cumbersome toolbox onto the platform. The run to New Street — Birmingham's main line station — was uneventful. It would be eleven thirty when I arrived and I was directed to the other side of the Bull Ring. There I was told I could catch a bus for Shirley.

The pub names were unfamiliar — 'Red Lion' and 'The Saracen's Head', as opposed to 'Quinn's Bar' and 'Slattery's Wines and Spirits'. My first British drink was a pint of Mitchell's and Butler mild — other pubs sold Ansells Ale. I drank my first pint rather fast and changed my pound note in the process. I quickly ordered another pint and chose to stand by the bar rather than take a seat. A darts match was in progress between a few people whose names were chalked on the board. I hadn't seen darts played before on this scale. Darts wasn't a popular game in Dublin. I stood there watching the goings on with interest.

'Care for a game Pat? … Pat, do you want a game?' (this time more urgently). I looked about for poor old Pat. He must be deaf. It soon dawned on me that 'Pat' was none other than 'Purdy'.

'I'm not very good at it,' I began, feeling a bit foolish under the gaze of dozens of Brummie eyeballs.

'That's OK, Pat, no worries. We're only playing for a tanner.'

'Right, right,' I said, now fortified by my third pint. I soon got into the swing of it and agreed with the others when hard luck was chorused or when 'Good shot' was in order. We lost a tanner, put our name down again and won a couple of tanners, lost again and so it went on.

I arrived at Brian's house after the pub closed. By now on a zig-zag course and the toolbox heavier than ever. My arrival was unexpected. My brother happened to be out, so it was a surprised sister-in-law Mary who greeted me at the door. I sat down to a typical Irish dinner, boiled bacon and cabbage, not one of my favourite dishes, nonetheless welcome under the circumstances. My brother duly arrived home and we sat swapping yarns for hours, I bringing him up-to-date on current affairs in Dublin, while he informed me of the best possible sites where work could be found.

Monday morning, I was out early. I hadn't walked any distance before spotting a large board nailed to some hoarding surrounding a building site. My heart leaped on reading the notice: 'carpenters and labourers required for immediate start.'

In the site agent's office I explained my predicament; being a shipwright, I said, would have its drawbacks until I got to know the local jargon. Shuttering he said is 'Bugger all, can you use the tools?'

'Yes sir,' I replied, hastily.

'When can you start?'

'Today,' I blurted, unable to control my excitement.

'Go get your tools,' he said, turning back to study a drawing in front of him.

It was strange at first, grappling with the Brummie dialect, and the various names which applied to certain jobs. However, I coped and it worked! There was overtime as well which suited me. I was out to earn money. My first pay day approached with mounting joy and fulfilment. From the corner of my eye I watched the foreman make his way round the site handing out fat healthy pay packets. Soon he was by my side. I'd waited twenty-one years for this moment. My first real pay packet with a realistic amount inside.

'Yours, Pat,' he said smiling, and moved on. I opened the packet with indecent haste. After stoppages I had nineteen pounds, the feeling was indescribable. I'd never in my whole life had that much money. I was overjoyed and counted it again and again, almost in disbelief.

We finished at five on pay day, which fell in with my plans. I'd noticed a tailor's shop in the vicinity and I was going to give myself a real treat. A suit made to measure, needless to say, my first. I proudly chose a blue pinstripe and put a ten pound deposit on it, another eleven pounds outstanding. Well my next pay packet would cover the balance. My next stop was the Post Office where I purchased a 'G' size registered envelope and sent two pounds home to my Ma. I continued to send this amount home each week, except when hard times made it impossible. My stay in Birmingham was less than a year — ten months in fact.

When I became accustomed to my surroundings I was surprised to sense an anti-Irish feeling. As this was my first contact with another race I felt annoyed. People seemed to look down on anyone or anything Irish. This wasn't just in my imagination. My opinion then that working class people, irrespective of creed, were on a par was to take many a jolt. Shock number one came when a girl's mother forbade me to see her daughter. It was painfully obvious that it was simply because I was Irish. On other occasions I was to see it on the vacancies board outside factories, 'No Irish Need Apply'. The same words were frequently printed in the local papers in the Situations Vacant column. It was easy to pick up an inferiority complex in this neck of the woods.

I became pals with two lads of my own age, both were Brummies. Browsing through the paper one day, over a pint, I noticed an advert looking for ore miners. The place was Canada. I discussed this with my pals and all three of us decided to take up the offer. We were sent to London for a medical, all expenses paid. I failed the medical, the same fate befell one of my pals, a lad called Frank. Edgar, the other buddy, passed and off he went to dig iron ore out of some distant Canadian mountain. I was never told the reason for my medical failure, nor indeed was Frank. Later, when I was an established seaman, I was to learn of Frank's death — by suicide.

Soon after the medical we returned to Birmingham. The hour was late and the last trolley bus had long departed. We'd all had enough to drink on the train and treated the five mile walk to Shirley as a morning stroll. Some way out of the city centre our high spirits got slightly out of control. I acquired a wheelbarrow, borrowed without the owner's consent from a small section of road which was under repair. It was agreed that we would take turns pushing while one or other reclined in the mud-caked conveyance. This happy state of affairs continued for a couple of miles. We were oblivious to the wear and tear on our clothes. Suddenly a police car cruised to a halt. At that particular moment it just happened to be me doing the pushing (worse luck). The usual line of questioning followed. Names and addresses were jotted down.

'Who actually took the barrow?'

I readily admitted my guilt. Frank and Edgar were given a stern warning as to their future behaviour, and I was ordered to take the wheelbarrow back. The police car followed me in slow gear until the mission was accomplished. I was then given a warning and of course had another two miles to travel. So much for a stupid prank.


My ultimate objective was, of course, to join the Merchant Navy and sail in the capacity of ship's carpenter. I had written to the British Shipping Federation then at Dock Street in Aldgate, East London. In due course, I received some forms to fill in. I gave them prompt and urgent priority. Eventually I was invited to visit the establishment pool for a medical! This visit, I was informed, would be purely at my own expense. A day absent from work without pay and a return ticket to Euston wasn't in my estimation an encouragement to people like me to become seafarers. I made the journey, and back in Birmingham eagerly awaited the result of the medical examination. When it did arrive I was to be bitterly disappointed. I'd failed, it seemed because I had a couple of bad molars. This made me absolutely furious. Why put a working man to all that expense just to tell him he had a couple of bad teeth. Surely it would have been kinder to inform all applicants to appear with a healthy set of teeth. In a fit of pique, I sat down and wrote a very ill-tempered letter to the Chief Registrar, telling him in no uncertain terms of my feelings. In the meantime, I had the offending molars extracted.

Birmingham and I were soon to part company. I honestly assumed that my chances of shipping out would be enhanced if I removed myself to the coast. Unfortunately, my time and choice wasn't a good one.

Once my mind was made up, I was off. Destination, Barrow-in-Furness. The large shipbuilding yard of Vickers Armstrong was the attraction. It is not a big port as such, for ocean going ships: a wiser choice would have been Liverpool. With Cammel Lairds just across the Mersey, even London or the Tyne, but no, stupid me, on a Sunday too, was chu-chuing it north to Barrow.

I had said my goodbyes to my few acquaintances in Birmingham and left New Street Station in an alcoholic haze. During my period of employment in Brum I could have saved some money for such a move, but, needless to say, I didn't. I was living it up. I was then your actual 'Jack the Lad'. I wasn't completely penniless however reaching Barrow. I managed to get myself a room. It was situated above a pub, rent three pounds a week, no problem there, assuming of course that I got employment at Vickers Yard.

It was now that mistake number two came into play. The date then was towards the latter end of July. Vickers Armstrong, I learned, was closed down for the annual holiday; it wouldn't open until the second week in August. I immediately realised my money wouldn't last. I cursed my stupid luck. Monday saw me walking around the town, slightly desperate, looking for a job of work — anything considered. Every conceivable avenue was explored, at least as much as one could fit into Monday and Tuesday. Actually, it was Thursday before I noticed it, I must have passed it several times on my ramblings. It was a small branch of the Shipping Federation. The office seemed to be run by a solitary official. He turned out to be a very pleasant and sympathetic chap and listened with patience as I related my current state of affairs. In short, I wanted to get to sea and he gave me my chance.

'No deep sea ships enter this harbour,' he warned, 'but it might be possible to get you shipped out from another port.'

I had another medical and was passed fit for sea duties. A visit to the Board of Trade was next on the agenda; here I was issued with an identity card and discharge book, Number R649177. By the following week, my funds were exhausted. I spent hours daily chatting to the official in the establishment office. It came home to me that seafaring wasn't very popular in Barrow. Not one other single applicant made an appearance during the days I spent there. Friday loomed, and my rent was due. Although the landlady at the pub was a kindly soul and her meals were well cooked and ample, the thought of having to tell her I was broke wasn't at all appealing. I would need at least a week's grace. What excuse could I offer, and why should she accept an excuse in lieu of payment? These thoughts and many more clouded my brain as I made my way yet again to the Merchant Navy Office. My financial circumstances were well-known to the official, I'd been bending his ear all week. His first act when I entered was to offer me a cigarette. He was smiling.

'You look cheerful,' I began, accepting the proffered smoke thankfully.

'There's a coaster in the harbour looking for a deckhand,' he said. 'Are you interested? It'll get you off the beach,' he continued, 'and you'll be earning wages too.'

Without hesitation my answer was firmly in the affirmative.

'Don't forget,' the official warned, 'when you do decide to pay off, be sure you choose a big shipping port.'

Admittedly a deckhand's rating would be entered in my discharge book, but this wasn't the time to worry about my carpenter's rating. By that evening I was a seaman. The Captain of the m/v *River Fisher* decided I would fit the part. The formality of signing home trade articles was completed at the Board of Trade office and I scrambled aboard late that night.

The *River Fisher* was six hundred tons. Her crew consisted of Master, Mate, Chief Engineer, Second Engineer, Cook-cum-Steward, Galley Boy and four Deck Hands. Battening down the hatch, spreading the canvas tarpaulins and placing wedges in the cleats, driving them home against the coamings, was nothing new to me.

We sailed for London, the only set back being I didn't have a Steering Ticket, which was no bonus for the other hands who would have to do all the watches on the wheel, especially entering and leaving port.

The Old Man was always good for a sub. The other sailors and I would go ashore at every given opportunity and invariably get inebriated. Our cargo varied from coal to cement. Cleaning and hosing down the hatch was a full-time occupation. The overtime earnings were good by the standards of the day. The other lads all had deep sea experience to their credit; their tales of the West

African coast and other distant parts of the globe were fascinating and held me spellbound. And they intoned more than once, I was wasting my time on a coaster.

'Go get your rating,' they urged often enough.

All this was undoubtedly good advice, but I was happy and content on this little ship. My belly was getting its fair share too, and what's more there was a jingle of coins in my pocket. One particular run was to Invergorden: I marvelled at the scenic side of Scotland, which was reminiscent of my hiking days to Pine Forest.

All together my total period of employment on the *River Fisher* was seven happy weeks. The highlight of the time spent on articles was a run to Rotterdam. It was 'abroad' for me then. And, of course, this entitled all the crew to bonded stores — two hundred cigarettes and a bottle of rum for me, and a run ashore in Holland.

On coastal articles a seaman had only to give eight hours notice to sign off. My chance came when we loaded a cargo for Middlesborough, just down the line from Newcastle. All hands believed my moment had arrived.

'Grab the bull by the balls,' they said. 'Any silly fucker can grab him by the horns.' Well that's debatable, to say the least!

I gave notice of my intentions with reluctance. It was hard to let go of the little security I'd found on the coaster. The friendship and companionship would be sadly missed too, but more money was in the offing with the proper rating, plus the big wide world out there. I paid off with approximately twelve pounds and made my way to Newcastle, later moving on to South Shields. Large deep-sea Whalers were at that period sailing out of the Tyne, the average round trip was two years. I toyed with the idea of going whaling, presuming of course that the opportunity presented itself. However, these romantic thoughts didn't prevail. I simply booked into 'The Flying Angel' for a couple of nights and went exploring the local pubs, mostly the haunts of seamen. The Geordies I found generous. They were good seamen too, as I was to discover on later voyages.

'The Dam', as the pool was known, was situated directly

behind the Mission to Seamen. So it was there the following morning I went, suitably armed with my discharge book, inscribed with a very good discharge for 'conduct' and 'ability' in the appropriate squares. In contrast to Barrow-in-Furness the pool at South Shields was a hive of activity. I pushed my way to the unestablished cubicle. An official listened patiently to my application for a berth as sea-going carpenter. On examining my discharge book a noticeable frown crossed his face.

'You'll have difficulty with this,' he said, indicating my recent discharge. 'It will hinder your chances. No Chief Officer is going to believe you're a chippy.' I produced my shipwright's clearance from The Workers' Union of Ireland. He studied the contents for some moments.

'That will help,' he intoned, 'but you still haven't any sea-going experience in that capacity. Anyway, there's nothing I can offer you today, show your face tomorrow.'

My few pounds would have to be stretched. It could be weeks before a position was found. Two days later found me back at the same desk, telling the official I would consider any position — even a deckhand — because another financial crisis was imminent. He searched through some cards with nicotine-stained fingers, eventually pausing at one.

'There's a tanker here, the *San Leonardo*, bound for Curacao; she's in ballast, signing on at two o'clock this afternoon.' He continued in response to my nodding head, 'There's no guarantee that the mate will accept you, he's requested able-bodied men,' he warned.

'I'll take it,' I said excitedly. The Dutch West Indies immediately sparked off dreams of 'doubloons', pirates and pieces of eight.

'Don't build your hopes on getting a berth,' he insisted.

But alas, I already had. Taking the proposed form, I left the pool with a feeling that my present difficulties and problems had been solved. A pub called 'The Willie Woodhalf' was adjacent to the pool and it was to there that I retired to celebrate and contemplate swaying palms and grass-skirted girls. Not too much to drink, I decided, wanting to appear smart and sober.

At the Board of Trade office the ceremony of signing on articles had to be taken seriously, especially by my goodself, whose position was precarious. The office was fairly busy, obviously the other seamen crowding the room were, or would be, the rest of the crew. Three men were positioned behind the large mahogany counter. The Shipping Master, the Ship's Captain and the First Mate. The Mate was tall and slim. I assumed him to be in his mid-thirties. He was busy examining the ratings' discharge books, each one deliberately in turn. A nod of his head was the seaman's cue to move along to the Old Man. A ledger was then placed in front of him. Once he signed, he was duly committed to complete the voyage. I gradually moved forward, growing more confident with each move. Soon it was my turn. I tried to explain as hastily as I could my usual particulars or, rather, lack of them.

The Mate soon had my 'book' in his hands, flicking over the empty pages at what I considered an alarming rate. Looking me straight in the eye, he snapped, 'You're not required. Next!' he called, and my Discharge Book clattered back on the polished counter.

'Next! 'he barked again. This time a note of impatience could be detected in his voice.

I retrieved my book, crestfallen. A few sympathetic glances met me as I trudged out of the building into the weak Autumn sun. I hurried back to the pool with a certain amount of urgency in my steps. It would soon be closing its doors for the day and there was a remote possibility that another berth would present itself. I'd heard tales of pier-head jumps, this situation would arise from seamen deserting at zero hour, thus enabling the likes of myself to get a flyer. Seamen lounged in the vicinity of the mission, hoping that the powers that be would come a-running for replacements. Seamen with continuous bad discharges found it extremely difficult to 'ship out' and always dreamed of such happenings.

I arrived back at the pool with twenty minutes to spare. Present were a few 'diehards', undoubtedly hoping for a miracle. The pool official didn't seem unduly concerned when I told him of my misfortune. He simply shrugged his shoulders and said, 'Pop in tomorrow.'

I waited in vain until I was ejected and the doors were bolted. That night, I couldn't afford to go on the grog. I just threw myself out of shape in the foyer of the mission and generally listened to other seamen's tales of woe. Some were really in dire straits, without even a consoling cigarette. Who was I to complain? I retired to my small room early, better to sleep than brood. There was always tomorrow, one had to be optimistic, and I had plenty of optimism.

The following morning I washed my eggs and bacon down with several cups of sweet tea before putting a match to a smoke. I felt at peace with the world and somehow felt lucky. It was one of those feelings that I've experienced on several occasions since, and invariably they have proved correct.

I was one of the first to arrive at the pool, but it was soon filled to capacity with lots of eager seamen clamouring for jobs. The blue hazy smoke from numerous cigarettes stifled the cramped space. After declaring my presence, I positioned myself against the back wall. I chose this spot because I could be easily seen by the officials at the unestablished counter. The minutes merged into hours but somehow I was confident and my confidence and earlier premonition was to prove correct.

# Chapter 13

'Purdy!' My name was called loud and clear by the official. My ears shot forward; a randy donkey would have been envious at the sight. A few short strides and I was at the counter.

'You should get this one,' he began. 'A bulk carrier bound for Seven Islands, Canada, to load iron ore. Only a short one though. Coming straight back to the UK. Fancy it?'

'Need you ask?' I enthused, betraying my excitement.

'Only a deck hand's job,' he pointed out good humouredly.

'Only too pleased to accept,' I countered.

'She's signing articles on board, get your tail along to the docks and see the mate.'

My eyes feasted on the *Stanbell*. She was a converted tanker. I noticed her catwalk was still in existence. I climbed the gangway and made my way to the centrecastle and the Chief Officer's cabin. I was surprised to meet an elderly man with three gold braid rings. At a guess, I'd say he wasn't far off retiring age. Apparently opportunity and promotion had left him astern. He seemed a nice friendly sort of person an listened with patience as I related my tale of woe once again. I was beginning to get bored, relating the same old line myself. Then, much to my delight, I heard him say: 'That's OK son, we're signing on at three-thirty, come back then and bring your gear with you.'

Jubilant was the word. Canada! Really going abroad! Back at the pool the doctor passed me fit. I collected my belongings from The Flying Angel, leaving my toolbox at the Left Luggage Office.

My cabin on the *Stanbell* was a double berth. I shared it with another sailor who was, in fact, a senior Ordinary Seaman from

Jarrow. After signing articles, the rest of the evening was our own. I requested and received a split note on the owners for five pounds. I got it cashed by one of the many money sharks who lurked around the docks. He charged twelve shillings and six-pence commission for the privilege. The 'shark', or commission agent, would collect the full five pounds when the ship sailed. A lot of money was to be made by the few.

I turned to for duty the next morning at 7 o'clock, feeling the worse for wear. It soon wore off once I hit the deck and gulped down some fresh air. 'The Blue Peter' was flying aloft, sig-nalling the fact that the ship would sail within twenty-four hours.

Breakfast on my first ocean-going ship was excellent, in fact sumptuous! I was pleasantly surprised at the choice of menu, which included cereals, porridge, beef curry and rice, eggs, bacon, waffles and syrup.

After dining, it was all hands on deck to prepare for sea. We sailed at noon. My station was on the fo'c'sle head, the windlass cranked into life and the moorings were singled up to a back spring and a head rope. Finally, the order rang out from the Bridge, 'Let go fore and aft'. The final moorings were cast off and splashed noisily into the Tyne. I was elated. Underway at last, my deep sea career had begun.

The ropes and back springs were duly hauled on board and stowed in the lower peak, lest they be washed over the wall in a storm. We would be crossing the western ocean in ballast. The tugs hauled the *Stanbell* laboriously to midstream, before casting off. The ship's head slipped down the River Tyne. I didn't have any heavy weather gear, in fact my predicament was known to seamen as 'schooner rigged'. It became cold on deck as the Tyne was swallowed up. Everything movable on deck was secured.

Sailors respect the western ocean. The order to stand down came at two-thirty, watch keepers only on deck. The cold wind was cutting through me by now as the lay of the land surrendered its comparative shelter to the open sea.

'Smoko,' the Bosun cried. 'All hands to the Mess for a mug of tea.'

The warmth of the Mess was most welcome. I was detailed for

the four to eight Watch, which effectively meant I could sit in the Mess supping tea and smoking until then. It transpired that I was to be Farmer of the Watch, after cutting a deck of cards with the other sailors for First Wheel, etc. I could now take my turn at the helm. Watch duty rota was two hours lookout and although it was a favourite spot, I wasn't over the moon with the idea, knowing full well my deep sea gear was not only inadequate — it was non-existent. Being close to land didn't help, as the lookout station was on the f'c'sle head. Shipping traffic was very heavy. I rang the bell noisily, warning the Bridge of ships in the area. Being Farmer, my finishing time was seven. My only other duty then was to call the eight to twelve Watch and make sure a pot of tea was made ready for those turning to. Having done this, I immediately had a hot shower and retired to my bunk.

The top bunk had been allocated to me. I climbed up and in. Others no doubt would be on Watch until my turn came around again at four the following morning. In the meantime I let the churning screws lull me to blissful warmth and ever-so-easy sleep. I didn't stir an inch until a voice from the Dogwatch jarred me to wakefulness.

'It's three thirty Paddy!' The cabin door closed and he was gone. I tumbled sleepily from the bunk, realising I was 'Deep Sea' and had duties to perform.

The deck was dark when I ventured out to do my stint on the wheel. The *Stanbell* was now under a full head of steam and well out to sea. Making my way to the Bridge I entered its dark interior on the stroke of eight bells. The small green light of the gyro compass was the only sign of life. I felt my way in the direction of the wheel and relieved the man on duty, calling out in a loud voice the course which was dictated to me by the Helmsman. It was answered by the Mate and I settled down to my first monotonous hour steering a big ship.

The digital numbers of the compass danced in the inky darkness. The Mate loomed at frequent intervals to gaze over my shoulder, thus checking I was on course. It soon became apparent that the Mate was of a nervous disposition and would breathe more freely when the broad water of the Atlantic was reached. It didn't make it any easier for those on the wheel endeavouring to keep a ship in ballast on course. The Mate, glued to the wheel-house window, could see the bow and as soon as the head moved to port or starboard he's be back checking the compass. One or two degrees off course meant an instant ticking-off. I was glad to see my own relief arrive at five. I had visions of going ashore and living it up in Canada but, as the trip progressed, I was to learn that Seven Islands was out in the sticks and that we would be loaded by conveyor belt straight from the ore mine. It would be a quick turn around and quick it was.

The weather proved to be kind and my first crossing of the Atlantic was spent watch-keeping and sleeping (there was no overtime to be earned). On arrival we were actually alongside the berth twelve hours.

I walked down the gangway to stand on terra firma, I was determined to have it known that I had been ashore in Canada. I stood on Canadian soil for several minutes before climbing back on board feeling gratified.

We sailed at ten in the evening for the UK — destination Barry Dock, Cardiff. It was raining heavily. We cleared the quay fairly quickly but the exercise of having to stow the gear meant it was past midnight before we stood down. Needless to say, I was thoroughly soaked, my hair was matted to my head, the Watch was as you were. I soon had my gear off. After a hot shower I felt human again.

The duration of the voyage was three weeks. The *Stanbell* was due to dry dock for her annual overhaul, so it was a general pay off for all hands. This was a bitter blow to me. I'd been looking forward to doing a longer voyage on the vessel to enable me to save some money. My accumulated pay for the whole trip, including leave pay, was seventeen pounds plus a travel warrant back to the Tyne. Most of the crew were heading in the same direction.

It was well into the Autumn. I promised myself some warmer clothes. I went through the whole process of booking into the Mission; most of the other lads had homes to return to in the Tyne area — they were lucky. The fifteen shillings per night at

'The Flying Angel' was a big burden to shoulder with very limited resources.

My first night back at the Mission was certainly one to remember. I'd had several pints of grog in a local pub with another seaman. He was an able-bodied sailor and had been with me on the *Stanbell*. He was a Scot from Inverness. We had adjoining rooms at 'the Flying Angel' and it was to our respective rooms we staggered under-the-influence, having vowed to be friends for life, telling each other we would stick together through thick and thin. After bidding each other goodnight for the hundredth time, I slammed the door shut.

Undressing in a haphazard fashion, I crawled between the sheets. In no time I was asleep — out to the world. Soon I awoke, how much later I really can't tell, but I'd say within an hour of turning in. There was someone in the room. The bedclothes had been pulled back to my knees, and my little 'cory' was in the hand of the intruder. The lock on the door was a Yale-type affair, so whoever was in there was undoubtedly in possession of a pass key!

The light had been switched on. My brain was clouded with booze and some minutes elapsed before my eyes came to focus properly. They finally distinguished the shape at my bedside — it was the dog-collar that caught my eye. It was the Padre. I hastily pulled the bedclothes over my exposed and vulnerable parts and muttered 'Fuck off'. Oddly enough, he just turned and left the room, dowsing the light as he departed. I quickly fell into a deep sleep again. The following morning I showered and dressed and wondered had I experienced some sort of nightmare. Jock was up and about when I knocked at his door. He opened it to admit me, a fag dangling from his unshaven face and before I could open my mouth he said, 'Guess what?'

'My head isn't in any shape for guessing,' I said mournfully.

'The vicar,' he began, 'only tried to give me a gobble last night.' So I hadn't been dreaming after all. Jock's mouth sagged open when I told him of the visit I'd had.

'Hope he doesn't put it on the bill,' I offered by way of a joke.

'I've got a good mind to put one on his chin,' Jock replied.

'The dirty bastard will be preaching a sermon, downstairs in the chapel Sunday night.'

'Yes, telling us sinners to come and be saved,' I said.

'More likely to come and be serviced,' Jock replied laughingly.

'Are you having breakfast?' I said, changing the subject.

'No. The bible puncher has put me off breakfast,' Jock replied, rubbing his spent fag into an ashtray. 'You carry on,' he said, 'I'll see you later.'

In a matter of days we were broke. The small 'pay-off' was gone — all spent on grog. There was nothing down at the pool for me. However, Jock, being an able-bodied seaman, was soon offered work and, needless to say, he had to take it. He secured a berth on a tanker for the Persian Gulf. The last time we shook hands was a solemn affair. We were both sober and penniless but at least Jock had a berth.

'We'll keep shipping out of the Tyne,' Jock said without much conviction.

'Where else?' I said, averting my eyes. We were never to cross paths again.

I was to spend the next four days without a meal, a smoke, or a cup of tea. The tanker had sailed, taking Jock with it. A shaking and nodding of the head in the negative was the only response from the pool. I was still anxious to get my rating but the situation was more desperate than ever. I'd nowhere to sleep. I'd been told to get my head down in the Mission bathroom. Most of the seamen on the beach availed themselves of this unorthodox facility. Basically, there was nothing wrong with the idea. The whole Mission was centrally heated and the bath was better than the street. One could wash the following morning too, which helped.

I spent Thursday hanging about the pool — nothing doing. The mission closed its front doors at eleven thirty at night. Paying guests who arrived late simply went to the side entrance for admission. An old retired seaman was employed as night watchman. Latecomers knocked, gave a room number and were admitted. With seamen constantly coming and going, the watchman didn't know who was resident and who wasn't; he simply opened and closed the door. I waited outside until almost midnight before knocking. I was cold and miserable when the door swung open. I gave a fictitious room number with all the aplomb I could muster, said 'Goodnight' to the watchman, and climbed the stairs.

The line of bathrooms was situated on the first floor. The first one I entered was occupied, another seaman on the beach was stretched out and snoring peacefully. The second one was vacant. It was cosy and warm, the bath was nice and dry, removing my shoes I bundled a bath towel into a ball — this would suffice as a makeshift pillow. I lay down feeling the world wasn't such a bad place after all. I hadn't been prone for ten minutes when the door opened — there framed in the entrance stood the cock-sucking Padre.

'Come on,' he said, 'out! It's not a doss house.'

I felt like saying it wasn't God's house either, but decided against it. Instead I vacated the bath and pulled on my shoes. The occupant of the other bathroom was given similar treatment. The Padre followed us both downstairs.

'These two are non-residents,' his voice was cold and impersonal. The watchman merely nodded and opened the door. He was used to these impromptu evictions.

The cold night air took a bite as I hit the street. Pulling up my collar was a futile gesture. The other seaman swore loudly and moved off in search of other shelter. The next hour or so was spent walking up and down outside the Mission. After a while my legs ached. The wind whistled down the side street, adding to my acute discomfort. Finally, I took refuge back in the doorway and sat down tucking my hands under my short coat for warmth. As yet I'd no overcoat. I dozed for a while, but my position on the cold ground made sleep impossible.

Despair and hardship were nothing new to me, I was related to them both but I was getting fed up with their presence. The Assistance Board in those days was a far different cry from the Social Security we know today. A seaman in particular seemed to be singled out for special treatment. It was a complete waste of time and effort to approach these so-called government aid buildings. The assistance one received was nil, in fact you invariably left the office with a guilty conscience for being so spendthrift.

The first question to be asked was 'What was your last ship?' Then — 'How long did the trip last? How much pay-off did you receive? Can you produce your pay-off slip or account of wages? You mean to say you've actually spent all of that in such a short time?'

Never, of course, taking into consideration the amount of time spent away at sea earning it. Making up for lost time was considered silly. One's leave, no doubt, should be spent in a monastery or perhaps in 'The Flying Angel' having your cock licked. I'd long been of the opinion that what defines class is money. A lord is a tramp without it, a tramp is a lord with it.

Suddenly the door opened, the watchman beckoned me in. 'You'll catch your death there,' he intoned. 'Look, get your head down on the settee.' He pointed to a long cushioned form in the Games Room.

'You'll have to be gone by six thirty, the Vicar will be up and about by then.' Having said my thanks with a firm promise to be gone at the allocated time, I removed my shoes. My feet were like blocks of ice, but the general warmth of the place soon lulled me to sleep. It seemed only minutes before the watchman was calling me again. 'It's just gone six,' he whispered. 'Get yourself a scrub and be off.'

After washing I thanked my saviour more fully.

'Come back tonight,' he said, 'if you don't get a ship. But not before midnight. The cock-sucker sometimes wanders about 'til then.' So the watchman knew the Padre too!

'You're a pal,' I said, feeling revitalised. I let myself out into the early morning air, the pool wouldn't be open until nine. Two and a half hours roaming about South Shields on an empty stomach wasn't my idea of heaven, but what state would I have been in sleeping rough?

All day was spent in the pool never giving up hope of getting a berth. The doors closed at four — still no work. The situation was desperate. Not a friend in sight. Saturday the pool would be open for half a day, but today, Friday, was still young. Saturday was a long way off. The hours passed with agonising slowness. Today had to be faced, tomorrow could fend for itself. I drank lots and lots of water to stave off my hunger.

Saturday's search for a ship proved fruitless. I'd now to face the daunting prospect of a whole weekend without food. After two days, the hunger pangs had worn off; just an emptiness and a little dizziness remained. Sunday was the ultimate in despair. The town was deserted, I wandered aimlessly to Jarrow then back to South Shields, the early hours were painstaking, not a soul to be seen. The Sabbath passed in a blur, longing for a job, longing for a meal, longing for a smoke, longing for comfort and an end to my misery. I vowed to myself over and over again that I'd never be in this predicament ever, ever again.

By Monday I was almost past caring. The Mission door closed behind me. There was no point in walking about, I hadn't the energy anyway. At eight-thirty I was still standing outside, not having budged an inch. Footsteps approached; the official from the unestablished counter of the pool was on his way to work.

'Good morning sir,' I said flatly as he passed.

He greeted me airily and waved. He appeared well fed and clothed. How I looked to him was another matter. I must have been a pretty grim sight indeed. I watched his retreating figure falter and pause. He stopped. Turning, he walked slowly back to where I stood. 'Are things that bad?' he said with genuine sympathy.

'I'm afraid so, sir,' I croaked. 'I've had nothing to eat these last four days.'

'Christ!' he whistled. 'As bad as that?' I nodded.

'You're a ship's chippy, aren't you?'

I nodded again. He pursed his lips before commencing. 'There's a ship,' he began. 'She's in Smith's Dock, she's looking for a full crew, including a carpenter. Come in and see me at nine. The job's yours.' He turned abruptly and continued on his way down the Dam.

Words of thanks poured from my lips and followed him with life-saving gratitude. I could have kissed the ground he walked on with pure and utter relief. New energy coursed through my body from some hidden source. Immediately my hopes soared to delight, the happiness that enveloped me was bliss beyond compare. A carpenter's berth too!

I'd arrived. The ship was the *Baron Renfrew*, bound for Cuba in ballast. The captain was James Bailey, a small wiry Scotsman. He was a little dubious when he examined my book, but I was not to be denied this opportunity. I produced my Shipwright's Clearance from The Workers' Union of Ireland. Words, convincing words, rattled from my mouth with positive emphasis on my ability. He looked at the Chief Officer.

'What do you think, Mr Mate?' he queried. My fate lay in the balance. My eyes never left the Mate's face. He studied me in return. It was only a matter of seconds.

'He'll do,' the Mate answered. Music, pure music. That reply meant salvation to me, in the true sense of the word.

'Sign here.' My name went down on The Articles.

'Any allotment?'

'Yes, two pounds weekly.'

'To whom?'

'My mother.'

'Monthly pay thirty five pounds. Any advance?'

'Please.'

'Amount.'

'Five pounds.'

The signing-on process was completed by noon. Galloping ashore I quickly cashed my split note. A restaurant was my port of call. A beef curry was polished off. Twenty smokes were purchased and the previous four days were unceremoniously forgotten.

The *Baron Renfrew* was a small ship of three thousand tons. She was built in 1933 and was known to the engine room crew as an up and down job — this being a reference to the large pistons which pumped up and down. She belonged to a company called Harold Hogarth. To seamen they were known as Baron Boats. They didn't have a good name for over-feeding the crew. The house flag was a double 'H' which some said stood for Health and Happiness; others preferred 'Hungry Hogarth'. Well, four days on the beach without a bite or a smoke and they meant 'Heaven's Here', and heaven it was for me anyway.

My own little cabin stood on the poop deck. I stowed my gear first before taking my tools to the Carpenters' Shop, which I found situated under the fo'c'sle head. That evening the meal was Lancashire Hot Pot. I had two large helpings, followed by large slices of bread and jam; then a shower and a run ashore with some of the crew for a few wets.

Being called 'Chippy' was like being hailed as 'Your Majesty'. The feeling was great. I slept soundly, nice and snug in my bunk. The following day we were off to Cuba. Warm weather the other side of the Azores, I was informed, and, boy, was I looking forward to every minute of it!

We sailed on schedule. The Tyne once again slipped by. Our little tramp was outward-bound. I didn't know then that I would not see the Tyne again in my Deep Sea career. Such was the life of a seaman who was unestablished. So much for 'We'll meet again' and the folklore surrounding the inevitable parting as ships docked and paid off.

Most of my work for the first week was down the lower hold of the various hatches. The ship's speed should have been ten knots. Perhaps in her hey-day such a speed was achieved,but now she was an old lady and well past her prime. The years had taken their toll.

We plugged on our way, reaching a top speed of eight. The *Baron Renfrew* was a sturdy ship, she performed well in adverse weather and I came to respect her and felt secure in the storms that lay ahead. After the Azores was astern, the change in temperature was remarkable. One day we were shivering on deck and the following day our shirts were off, enjoying the splendours and relaxed atmosphere that sunshine can bring. I particularly enjoyed the evenings.

The Bosun, now in his twilight years, was a Geordie. He had been a seafarer since the turn of the century. We were rationed on beer — two cans of McEwans daily the Master had decreed, at a shilling a can. It was served from the ship's fridge, ice-cold at midday. If you didn't want to drink it straight away you could wrap it in a blanket until evening. It would still be cold. Of course, this only applied to South of the Azores. The water from the ship's tank would get warm and tasted dreadful. A mug of cold tea was preferable to the aqua. Other sailors had their own ideas. They would save their daily allowance of beer and have a mini rave-up on Saturday night. The Bosun drank his immediately.

'Could be dead by tonight,' was his argument.

Many a warm evening was spent reminiscing sitting out on the hatch. The old Bosun was nearing the end of his sea-going days as well as his life. He was seventy then. He has long since gone to his final anchorage. His yarns and tales of long past voyages were a source of comfort and deep contentment to a very over-awed young man who was just commencing his Deep Sea career.

The Bosun had completed trips of three years' duration. 'Never worry about the length of the trip, when you sign on the Articles,' he intoned, 'because your hand will soon be back on the same Articles signing off. You listen to me Chippy, I'm a homeward bounder in the true sense of the word. One day your years at sea will end too. Yes, they'll hang suspended for a while, like drips from a leaking tap, the leak will get worse, the drips will quicken, so too will your years — sucked into a vacuum to be washed down and out of the scuppers.'

He went on reminiscing. 'In the days of sail and tall masts, the young sailors amused themselves when becalmed by racing each other up and over the rigging, no radio either. If you got into trouble, and if you were short of water a bucket hanging upside down from a yardarm was the signal to other ships of your plight.'

'Were they better men, Bosun?'

'No, just less fortunate. If you stay at sea, say 'til you're seventy like me, you will witness the great changes that will surely come and look back on this tramp as I look back on sail.'

'What was the longest voyage you did Bosun?'

'Thirty-nine months on a tramp steamer.'

'Is there anywhere you haven't been?'

'Yes, heaven, but the law of averages says I'll be signing on for that voyage in the near future.'

He reflected for a while and cleaned his pipe, tapping it gently on the hatch coaming. 'I bet that will be a long one,' he said with finality.

We arrived off Cuba — Santa Maria — and dropped the hook. There was no harbour. The water was shallow. Flat bottomed barges transported the sacks of brown sugar to the ship. The dockers arrived and actually lived on board the ship, sleeping on deck for the duration of the period it took to load. They had their own cook and utensils. A quantity of live chickens were left to run freely around the deck. A batch of them would be killed daily. (It's just another way of keeping meat fresh.) The dockers were a happy lot and played dice by night and drank lots of rum. Our semi-dry status came to an end. The docker's cook was the source of our now plentiful supply of grog. Bacardi, three bottles for an English white shirt or ship's grey blanket. The ship's blankets disappeared rapidly and the crew's knees buckled as fast.

A jolly boat was laid on for those wishing to hit the beach, and needless to say, we all wanted to hit the beach. Saturday lunchtime was my zero hour — finished until Monday. I was armed with an ample supply of pesos. I stood with mounting excitement aboard the jolly boat as the blurred outline of the shore took shape. The boat edged into some steps, my legs felt oddly light mounting the steps to the quayside. It was almost three weeks since leaving the Tyne. The strange feeling of firm and stable ground was a new chapter unfolding.

Small groups of people watched us with a detached air. New words and phrases I'd picked up en route were 'cows' (a loose word for prostitute), and 'bagging off' or 'getting your end away' (which don't need any explaining in these pages). What does need a little explanation is the fact that I was still uninitiated — a 'cherry' or virgin, call it what you will. This state of affairs was kept secret from the rest of the crew for obvious reasons. The score would be settled here in Cuba. I'd promised myself at the age of twenty-two that caution would go to the wind — take the plunge. But first a little drop of something to calm my fears and

doubts. Other men I knew were better shaped and more pro-
portioned than me. This had become patently obvious during the
last couple of years. There were other underlying facts too which
would emerge before the day was out. Later in life I would label
my condition simply as 'constricted penis'.

The main street ashore was a white, dusty affair; on a par with
a Wild West town. Men on horseback too, yelling and spurring
their mounts to greater effort; coming in, no doubt, for a dirty
weekend from the outlying sugar plantations. I was relieved to
see they weren't sporting six-guns strapped to their sides, and for
a few fleeting moments had visions of El Gringo from Dublin
being blasted into eternity.

There were plenty of bars open for business. 'Una-Servaza, mi
amigo!'

No shortage here. A ship in port was a special occasion. The
juke-boxes blared into the hot afternoon. 'Besa-mi, Besa-mi —
mucho' seemed to be popular. By evenings it wasn't the girls
who wanted picking up, it was the sailors; some of whom were
by now legless. The bar I'd chosen was big and airy. The old
Bosun had given me a few words of advice one evening, while
having our nightly chat on the hatch. He talked tirelessly and
endlessly, while I listened.

'Never go for the good-looker — the ravers — they will be
well serviced, in great demand at all times. Pick yourself a plain
woman, an older one preferably. She'll have had less attention.
She will know what she's doing and be less likely to be carrying
a dose. Even with penicillin it's a messy business.'

So here in the bar, a rum and coke in my hand and another on
the table, sat yours truly with the woman of his choice. She
seemed determined to prevent me from drinking too much. Her
age would be, at a guess, trienta cinqo.

The time arrived finally for me to take the plunge. I allowed
myself to be led off to a room, a small bamboo-type room, set
back from a wooden veranda. She spoke very little English and
my Spanish then was non-existent. Castro was out in the hills,
fighting for what would be his ultimate victory; and here I was,
lying in a single bed in Santa Maria, fighting my shyness.

It was painfully obvious that my small endowment was not rising to the occasion. My patient and experienced partner, to her eternal credit, never tired. She made various sexual advances, all seemingly to no avail. Finally she removed the half slip she was wearing and pulled it over my legs up around my waist. I immediately got an erection. She said 'Ah' and smiled, adding, 'Mi Chicko!'

It was a lovely sensual feeling and thereafter I made up for lost time. We spent the whole weekend together in a whirl of romance, generously abetted by rum and coke. However, one fact emerged from all this — I was 'kinky'. It was gratifying to learn some years later, on reading an article in *The Daily Mirror* by the famous Marjorie Proops who proclaimed (after an irate wife had written to the *Mirror* asking her advice regarding her husband — who, it appeared, enjoyed the same type of sex).

'One man in every four uses this method to gain fulfilment,' Marge wrote, and went on to say, 'Any means is fair, providing both partners agree.'

Fair comment!

I spent the following weekend again with my new found love, plus a couple of nights through the week. I borrowed as much money as the Captain would allow, endeavouring to give my first love all I could afford. The *Baron Renfrew* was down to her plimsoll line after ten days of hard work by our lodgers, the dockers.

The leaving was a sad occasion, but we were underway — homeward bound for London — Greenwich Buoys. I didn't know then, but I would never sail on a ship again that would call at Santa Maria, much to my lasting regret.

'Adios Mi Amigo', and as a famous line goes … 'If this be forever, then forever fare-de-well.'

Having passed the Azores homeward, I encountered my first real storm. Seas that I'd never thought possible crashed over our struggling little ship. Looking up from the trough was like looking at a towering mountain, but the little ship, which I now respected, would climb bravely to reach the pinnacle, only to catch the last ten or twelve feet of the angry waves that would sweep the fore-deck and all before it. Life-lines were stretched fore and aft for the safety of our crew. The Galley was midships, which meant meals had to be carried aft to the Mess. This thankless job fell to 'The Peggy', whose rating on board ship was Deck-Boy. In foul weather it was extra hazardous to carry the meals, hold the life-line and generally keep your balance.

The engine, in situations such as we were experiencing was shut in. Headway was down to three knots. Most of the crew were thoroughly fed up with their lot. To cover seventy miles a day wasn't awe inspiring. All agreed, however, on one thing, when they reached London they were paying off and not signing on again. A cadet had made the rounds, armed with a notebook, asking all hands if they would like to do another voyage. 'Purdy' was the only name on the list. There was plenty of advice coming my way from all quarters. All agreed I was mad to sign on for another voyage.

'The next trip might be eighteen months Chippy. Imagine being on this tub for a year and a half!'

My answer was firm and to the point. 'I'm doing another one.'

The conditions on the tramp didn't worry me. I'd been on the beach and didn't like it. Three fair meals a day, plus pay, and a snug little cabin was preferable to what I'd been through. I knew the ship too, which made life easier. A cushier carpenter's job would never come my way again. In those days I was most definitely an extrovert and would chatter away like a ventriloquist's dummy, asking and answering the questions. It took a long time to realise that I was just a bore. The realisation was sobering. The only words I heard were 'Yes Jim. No Jim. Yes Jim. No Jim.' Thereafter I shut my mouth and became an introvert.

After a bitterly cold stint at stations, sailing up the Thames, we reached Greenwich. I said my goodbyes to all my Geordie friends (including the Bosun). The voyage had lasted two months. My pay-off, after stoppages, amounted to twenty-seven pounds. A duffle coat, oil-skins and rubber boots were required, plus a warm Southwester. These items were purchased. I still had plenty left for a couple of runs ashore.

The next crew came from Dock Street pool — a street in the heart of London's East End. They seemed a good-natured lot and, indeed, turned out to be just that. We slipped the cable from the buoys and headed seaward, outward bound, for the Dominican Republic. It was back to the Caribbean via, you've guessed, the Azores. This time I was wrapped up, prepared for the elements. We were to load another cargo of sugar and sail back to London.

We arrived at Barahona and tied up alongside a jetty. This small country was then run by a dictator called Trujello — who ruled with great severity. The whole population seemed to be in a state of terror; corruption was rife too. Armed guards, with sten-guns, roamed the streets. Going ashore meant taking two packets of smokes: one for the guard on the gangway and the other twenty for yourself. One evening I cleared a bar by saying, by way of conversation, 'Trujello must be a proper bastard.' The mere mention of El Presidente's name was enough to send the locals scurrying from the bar en mass into the warmth of the evening. Trujello's reign was ended by an assassin's bullet (not surprising either!).

The process of loading began; the heavy sacks of sugar arrived by rail car, the tracks reaching to the end of the jetty. Apart from the guards, going ashore was much easier than being at anchor, where one was committed to the comings and goings of the jolly boat. Walking around the town one evening in the company of a shipmate, we were accosted by a youngster who was no more than ten or eleven years of age. He was ragged and barefooted.

'You want to fuk my see-s-ter, Johnny?' he asked pleadingly.

The shipmate by my side had been complaining. It seemed his knob was top-heavy and no doubt he wanted to shed some of its load.

'You fuk my see-s-ter?' the youngster asked again.

'Dos senorettas par mi e mi amigo.'

'Si senor,' the kid laughed. 'Una uthra. Si senor.'

'Come on Chippy, we're on. He has two sisters!'

'How much are they going to rush us for?' I queried, thinking solely of my pocket.

'Muchatto, quanta costa?'

'Trienta pesos.'

'Thirty smackers,' he replied grinning. 'Not bad. Only a short time though. Still that's good enough for me.'

We followed the kid into shanty town; our destination was a shack. Inside were two girls. They spoke rapid Spanish to the youngster, and glanced fearfully from the window.

'What did they say?' I whispered.

'Fuck knows,' was the instant reply.

'Listening to you back there gave me the impression you could speak Spanish.'

'Balls! Just a few necessary phrases.'

The room consisted of two well worn single beds; a matted cane screen was the partition which divided us. It kept us from shaking hands while doing our screwing. The girls were fairly well matched in terms of looks. They were clean and the shack harboured no obnoxious smells. Business was business — no time was lost in preliminaries. You could hear the other bed squeaking and rattling. My buddy was getting value for his pesos; my own contribution was slow off the mark. However, the senorita was well aware of such setbacks and soon had the situation under control. After a sensuous minute or two we were back on the dusty sidewalk.

'I kept going after the first one,' my buddy glowed enthusiastically. 'Two for the price of one.'

'I'd a gobble,' I said with the air of a man who was gobbled daily.

'A gobble!' he exclaimed. 'You lucky blighter.'

There was very little overtime on the *Baron Renfrew*. Being a day worker meant Saturday lunchtime to Monday morning was free time for the Chippy. In the warm weather I'd lie on the after hatch, taking the sun. The slow roll of the laden ship would dull one's senses. You could hear the quadrant rumble in the steering flat answering a call from the helm getting back on course. These were beautiful calm evenings and serene days. A few feather canyons flitting through the blue skies, 'way aloft', lulled one into a deep sense of well-being. Yet, not very far away, a hurricane had ripped through this same sea to claim eighty lives, and sink the German navy's training auxiliary *The Pamir* — five survived. We had picked up the urgent May-Day calls for assistance. There were other faster ships in the vicinity, but not near enough to save the majority of crew who perished in the turmoil. Lying there on the hatch it just didn't seem possible that the sea could raise its ugly head and sweep so many young lives to a watery and premature grave. Yet the sea, so unpredictable, did just that at intervals of violent turbulence.

I turned over on my back to let the warm sun toast my skin to a deeper brown. Close to home we picked up a general radio message to keep a lookout for another ship en route from Philadelphia to Brest with a cargo of coal — *The Nordic Star*. It wasn't on our course. She vanished with all hands. These things happened occasionally when ships were hit by a freak sea. A wave would swoop down on a ship while it was dipping and plunging its way through the normal rhythm of waves — one extra was too many. There was always the danger of ships capsizing too. Those with vulnerable cargoes like grain — which would shift to one side suddenly, giving the crew no chance to put matters right.

We docked at Dagenham on this second voyage and once again the whole crew paid off except me. They, too, were unanimous in their desire to leave 'Baron boats' to other sea-going mortals. I was just as determined to soldier on. Another crew from Cockney land signed on for this my third voyage. Imagine by delight when orders were received to proceed to Cuba for yet another cargo of sugar. My excitement was short-lived. Santa Maria was not to be the port of call. Two other small ports were designated; part cargo in each and both anchor jobs. We had the usual invasion of dockers sleeping on board, and jolly boats for the inevitable run ashore.

Barges again ferried the sugar to the ship. The sacks were simply emptied down the hatch. When a large amount had accumulated in the lower hold, down went the dockers to trim it into the four corners with big wide shovels. West India dock terminated our third trip. Another mass exodus from the crew ensued.

I now felt in need of a break and duly approached the Old Man. Captain James Bailey was a man that I hadn't seen much of during the past three voyages, but when our paths did cross, whether by accident or by order of command, I always found him courteous. Having already agreed and signed Articles for the next voyage it was, I suppose, asking a lot for leave with pay. My intentions were to travel home to Dublin to see the family. It was almost two years since I had emigrated. Captain Bailey pointed out in his soft Scots burr that being a small ship the dockers would make short shrift of unloading the vessel. For my part I said one day and a night would suffice. He reluctantly agreed and homeward bound I was.

This was a rather foolish and stupid mistake on my part. Flying home was out of the question because of the expense. Getting to Euston and catching the overnight train and ferry to Dunlaoghaire actually meant the night was gone, leaving only the day.

I should have travelled back that same evening. I didn't. I blissfully celebrated by homecoming by spending the day and night drinking grog. Buying it for all and sundry! I was told all too often I was looking well, and asked frequently when was I going back. The time passed too quickly. I boarded the ferry in an alcoholic haze. First to Holyhead, then the train and Euston. A big shock awaited me at West India Dock. The berth was empty. I looked again and again but my eyes were not deceiving me. Had she gone to another berth? Gone to anchor in the river? These thoughts and many more clouded an already clouded head. I retraced my steps to the Dock gates. The policeman on duty confirmed my worst fears — the *Baron Renfrew* had sailed at four thirty that morning. Dazed and bewildered, I stood there not wanting to believe the policeman.

'She waited a half hour for you,' he offered by way of consolation. 'Had to catch the tide though. Where the hell were you?'

'Travelling back from Dublin.' My words sounded hollow.

'Bad luck Paddy,' he mumbled, turning to answer the 'phone which was ringing urgently in his hut.

An overnight bag with a few odds and sods stuffed inside was all I had. In my pocket was fourpence. On the beach again! I shivered involuntarily. At nine o'clock the Board of Trade Office opened. I went there in the hope of retrieving my discharge book. It was there, having been brought ashore just before the ship sailed. Captain Bailey had entered 'Failed to join' in the left-hand corner. The shipping master had scrawled a censure mark across this and entered 'Voyage not completed'. This was, in fact, classified as a bad discharge. Another stunning blow to my sagging morale. The shipping master also informed me that the ship was bound for Newfoundland — Wabana in ballast — to load iron ore for the United Kingdom. The port of discharge yet to be decided. He assumed the ship would be back home within a month. My clothes and tools were on board. It seemed I would have to go labouring for a month, but first I had to have a roof over my head. Just up the road was the British Sailor's Society 'Home for Seamen'. It was fondly known as the 'Stack of Bricks'. The building still stands today, although not as a mission. It was through these doors I dragged my weary frame, cursing myself for taking leave and spending my money frivolously, especially after the eye opening hardship I'd suffered on the Tyne.

I entered the Padre's spacious office. He was a tall thin man in his thirties. A man no doubt who had seen many down and outs standing grovelling before him. My story was short and to the point. He asked to see my book. He seemed impressed when he'd seen I'd completed three previous voyages on the same vessel. He agreed to give me two free nights, bed and breakfast. This kind offer was graciously accepted and the pressing problem of accommodation was lifted temporarily. I accepted the key to my new-found sanctuary along with two tickets, one for each morning's breakfast. I asked and was given directions as to the whereabouts of Dock Street pool. No time was wasted legging it to Aldgate. It was crowded. The hungry, haunted looks of down and out seamen pressed to the counter. The SS Salvation was a ship that was always on the horizon. Hope and faith were in abundance. I thrust my book under the grid with a hurried explanation.

'A coaster for a month or two — anything,' I pleaded. The Federation Officer flicked open the pages, stopping at my last discharge. Closing it, he pushed it back. 'Sorry. Can't help you. Next!' I was pushed aside as another hopeful elbowed his way to disappointment.

Across the road from this depot of despair was 'The Red Ensign Club'. It was warm inside. The daily papers were free, open to all bona fide seamen and, being just that, I entered. The Red Ensign Club was the 'in' thing. It was residential, licensed, had large games rooms, shop, cafeteria, plus other favourable amenities. The day passed in comparative comfort. Sitting and telling all who wanted to listen and insisting on telling those who didn't want to listen, my misfortune. Others didn't have problems, if they did I wasn't interested. I was far too preoccupied with my own little patch. Three of the four pence I had was invested in a cup of tea.

As evening approached I moved back towards the Stack of Bricks. A book borrowed from the library and then my bunk. The book I chose didn't hold my interest for long but I was thankful for the free bed. Dousing the light to sleep was only a temporary solution to my problem.

The next morning my head was clear and a refreshing shower accentuated my hunger. The dining hall was busy, in fact, a small queue led to the distribution point. A young girl was collecting the tickets — you got egg and beans in return.

It was only then that I noticed that my ticket was a different colour from the others being handed in. My status at the Mission was noticed at a glance, it was a sobering thought. Charity had its embarrassing drawbacks, the breakfast somehow lost its flavour. I felt that prying eyes were on my every mouthful — a beggar in the midst of so many paying guests.

I left the dining hall rather self-consciously and started off in the direction of Aldgate. I'd noticed a couple of building sites in the vicinity of Whitechapel the previous evening and although I knew almost nothing about labouring work, I was confident I'd get a job, my accent was my passport.

The Red Ensign Club was my first stop, read the papers first and give the pool another whirl. Picking up the *Daily Express* I scanned the front page. A small, boxlike, news item caught my eye, sitting well down in column four. It stated 'Captain of Ocean Going Liner Dies'. I wasn't really interested in captains of big ships and my attention went elsewhere on the page. However, my eyes were drawn back to the item of news, it read as follows: 'Captain James Bailey of the ten thousand ton liner *Baron Renfrew* was found dead early today in his cabin.' Then it went on to say that the ship was proceeding to Swansea Roads to put his body ashore. It was unbelievable. The Old Man had died of natural causes. Then shock number two arrived. Turning to a seaman similarly engaged, his head deep in a newspaper, I said excitedly: 'See that, look there.' My finger pointing to the column. 'That's the ship I missed yesterday morning.'

'Well, you're laughing cock ain't you? Hungry Hogard has an office down the road. Get down there and see them, cock. Go on, do yourself a favour.'

'But I thought their office was in Scotland?'

One in Aldgate, too, cock. What are you waiting for?'

'Yea, what am I waiting for?' The door and the steps of The Red Ensign Club were quickly left astern.

The office was small but it was open for business. A young man examined my discharge book. 'You want to rejoin her?' he asked.

'Certainly,' I gasped. 'All my gear is on board. Besides, I like the ship and I need the job.'

A travel warrant to Swansea was thrust in my hand. 'Can I have a little in advance for expenses?' I ventured, hopefully. 'I've only a penny to my name.'

A pound appeared as if by magic, to make my day utterly complete. I paused to buy a packet of smokes before rushing back to the Stack of Bricks to retrieve my few belongings.

A hotel in Swansea was booked for the new Captain and myself. The train journey from Paddington was uneventful. It was late evening by the time the hissing engine ground to a halt. The hotel was adjacent to the station. A meal was provided with the information that we had to be up and about to join the ship at two-thirty in the morning. We had, in fact, beaten the ship to Swansea. Tea and toast was served at this unearthly hour by a cheerful waitress. The Board of Trade office was especially opened to enable me to sign on. A tug boat waited in the harbour. It was to ferry both of us out to the roads and return with the mortal remains of Captain Bailey. My thoughts hadn't dwelt so much on his misfortune, as on my own unbelievable good luck.

We approached the *Baron Renfrew* from the starboard side. A Jacob's ladder dangled over the side to touch the water's edge. Reaching the deck, the Chief Officer's first words were, 'Chippy, am I glad to see you!' I hastily assured him that the feeling was mutual. My cabin was just as I'd left it. Changing into warm gear I re-emerged on deck. The tug was still alongside. Making my way to the Old Man's cabin, foolishly thinking the Mate would have taken residence there, I knocked and entered, stepping smartly over the weather step only to go sprawling. The place was in darkness. Feeling about I involuntarily put my hand on the cold face of Captain Bailey. The body was strapped into a strait jacket in readiness for going ashore. Leaving the cabin hurriedly, I stood for some minutes in the cross alleyway, a little shocked.

After speaking to the Mate, it became obvious why he was glad to see me. The fore peak bulkhead had sprung a rivet, and as a consequence the lower hold in number one hatch was flooded to a depth of eighteen inches — no real problem normally, but some of the bulk sugar carried on the previous voyage had seeped into the bilges and solidified around the strum box, meaning of course the bilge pump wouldn't function. Number one double bottom tank was fortunately ballast as was the fore peak. The water would have to be drained into the double bottom.

'Wait until we get away, Chips,' the Mate advised. 'Go get yourself a smoke.'

A derrick was topped to swing Captain Bailey's remains over

the side. A final parting, the blowing of steam whistles signalling the last farewell from both the tug and the *Baron Renfrew*. Adios Mi Capitano.

# Chapter 14

The steam on the windlass bubbled and hissed. The anchor came slowly home. Having secured anchors, the daunting prospect of tackling the hatch faced me. I dangled a torch from my neck with some sail twine and descended into the Tween Deck. I could hear the water rushing from port to starboard. I stripped naked and, armed with a ring spanner, descended to the lower hold. The extreme coldness of the water cut into my body with biting force. I knew the approximate position of the lid. My bare feet soon found the nuts that would have to be undone just enough to ease the lid slightly open, letting the water escape while preventing other debris from entering the double bottom. Having already alerted the engineers to take the head off number one, it only remained for me to undo the nuts — about two dozen of them!

Words could hardly describe the extreme cold which gripped my body. Several times I had to retreat to the ladder and climb out of the water, returning when the circulation began to cause pain. Slowly, one by one, the nuts were tackled. At times my head under water as the ship's movement pushed the sea water, like a giant pendulum, from port to starboard and vice versa.

Some of the nuts were stubborn, which meant lying back and using one's feet to get them started. Slowly, ever so slowly, the almost impossible was achieved. When all were loose, I realised that a nail bar and wedge would be required; the latter to hold the lid slightly above the tank top. This meant hurrying back to the main deck again.

The Carpenter's Shop was in the fore peak. No lights were permitted on the fore deck while the ship was underway. I groped in the darkness, 'til I found what I wanted. Soon the surplus water was gurgling into the double bottom tank.

With a sigh, I made for the Tween Deck. There I dropped my tools with a clatter. I climbed to the Main Deck and hurried aft, naked. My clothes were tucked under my arm. I reached the accommodation and the shower with some haste. I turned the mixture valve to hot. My two little round things were shrivelled like walnuts. It was with great difficulty that I held the soap, my fingers and toes ached so much. Such was life on a tramp steamer.

Making a mug of cocoa later in the Mess, with a towel draped round my middle, I noticed the clock. It read five forty-five. It wasn't worth turning in. Looking on the lee side, I was back in the comfort of my little cabin with three meals a day to look forward to, and my discharge book problem ironed out too. All things considered, in terms of luck, I was on the right side of plus.

The voyage continued with all hands agreeing unanimously that I was a jammy bastard. The banks of Newfoundland gave off their usual misty appearance as we approached at a steady seven knots. The winter's ice had thawed. Soon we were ploughing through pack ice. This hazard was unexpected and gave rise to concern. The engines were shut in as growlers or small icebergs were spotted. More lookouts were posted and I was ordered to keep a constant check on the bilges and tanks. We saw large and formidable icebergs, some in excess of two hundred feet. The main strategy in pack ice is to keep steaming into it; to stop means it simply gathers around the ship, effectively blocking the passage. I noticed, on looking over the bow, that an outside strake or plate was peeling back from the stem. I duly reported this fact to the Mate who examined the damage with the Old Man.

It was slowly dawning on all hands that the ship was in trouble. Progress was slow and the ice grew thicker. Suddenly the engine faded. The silence in the midst of the ice was eerie. The real damage was confined to the stern. The ice quickly gathered along the starboard side. It was decided to pump out the ballast from the after peak and other double bottoms abaft the beam.

'Bring her tail up for closer inspection,' was the order.

My job was simply to sound the tanks and indicate when they were empty. The crew readied a lifeboat for launching. The stern was raised as much as safety would permit. The powers that be were still unable to determine the extent of the damage. The Old Man decided to put the lifeboat in the water and inspect the stern from close quarters. The port after side was the only patch of sea to be seen. The boat would have to be manhandled across ice to this clear area. Pack ice now stretched to the horizon — North, South East and West.

Six men with mixed feelings were put down on this vast Arctic waste: the Captain, Chief Engineer, the Mate, Second Mate, Second Engineer and myself. None of the other occupants were unduly perturbed and I can say with all honesty that I wasn't either. Being in danger never entered my head, although the Second Mate did mention the fact that if anything was to happen to us in the lifeboat it would leave the *Baron Renfrew* without a deck officer or engineer. Neither the Third Mate nor the Third Engineer had a ticket. Yet I somehow felt that those looking anxiously over the side were in a safer position than we were. A painter was used by the sailors to tow us around the stern — it was all hands on deck now. An emergency, safety of the ship and all that jazz, meaning no overtime to be paid to the Watch below.

Six pairs of eyes surveyed the damage. One of the propeller blades was bent almost double and was effectively acting as a stopper against the rudder post. The ship didn't carry an acetylene torch or bottles, so the offending blade could not be straightened, nor could it be cut. A missing prop blade would throw the tunnel shaft off centre and seriously damage the engine, so we were now fair game for salvage. Rockets sailed into the sky to burst and scatter their urgent message for assistance. Two black balls dangled lazily above Monkey Island, situated at the topmost part of the Bridge — a warning to all ships in the area that we were not under our own power — the elements it appeared had won the battle though not yet the war.

It was rumoured that an Italian freighter was sinking just over the horizon. an ice-breaker sailed from Saint John's in answer to our SOS, we settled down to ride out our first night in the firm clutches of pack-ice.

It was three days later that the m/v *Montcalm* hove into sight. Her reinforced bows making short shrift of the ice which held us prisoner. Lines were thrown and secured, the large hawser which would be our towing spring was made fast to the bits. On the first snatch the hawser snapped. The backlash caused mild panic on the f'c'sle head. All concerned took evasive action from the snapping, swishing ends of wire which swept the deck. Another giant hawser was laboriously hauled on board and made fast. Sailors, taking no chances this time, crowded behind the windless for the little shelter it offered. We were duly towed to St John's and dry dock, under the guidance of a Lloyd's Surveyor and a Company Superintendent who had been flown out from the UK for the occasion. After only a couple of weeks at sea, it meant that the subs or advances on wages were strictly limited and the opportunity to have a good time ashore was curtailed. We were four days in St John's before sailing again to pick up our cargo. Being a small ship it was difficult to accept that the relatively small heap of ore in the lower hold was in fact our full quota and the ship was fully loaded.

The run home went smoothly — our destination Eccles, Manchester to discharge cargo then take the *Baron Renfrew* back through the ship canal to Birkenhead to dry dock for another more extensive overhaul. This effectively meant a general pay-off for all hands.

It was with mixed feelings that I boarded the ferry that would take me across the Mersey to Liverpool. The money subbed in St John's meant there was little for merry making in 'La pool'. I just about had enough left for a couple of nights' stay in Atlantic House, the Mission to Seamen. My quest for work was urgent. A tour of the many shipping companies' offices was high on the agenda for the following morning.

Cunard required a stand-by carpenter. This bit of good news sailed across the counter while I stood in the office having my book examined. I would have to work ashore making fenders while on stand-by, and I would have to be ready to ship out at a moment's notice. Was I interested? Needless to say, I was very interested and highly delighted. I was back amongst the earners.

The next days were spent wielding the adze and tapering the fenders. The site was a large rigging loft adjacent to the docks. The period ashore was happy and carefree. A nice pay packet every Thursday evening. I continued to live in Atlantic House at fifteen shillings a night, bed and breakfast. Another more pleasant duty was to relieve the Chippy on incoming Cunarders, 'working by' until they returned after a spell of leave. These days and nights would be spent living on board ship, thus saving me a considerable sum of money.

The day dawned when the readiness clause was put to the test. The shore foreman rushed in to the loft. He was a man who had spent a large slice of his life at sea. Twenty years alone spent on one of 'The Queens'.

'Go and get your gear,' he said breathlessly. 'There's a cab waiting outside. Hurry! You're sailing on the *Carenthia*. I was soon tearing through Liverpool, no explanation was required at Atlantic House. They were more than used to this sort of rush and dash. The *Carenthia* was a passenger ship on the immigrant run to Canada, Quebec and Montreal. Five days outward, three days on the coast, and five days homeward.

The short notice worried me a little. I'd absolutely no time to get to know the ship. The *Carenthia* was twenty-two thousand tons, carrying a thousand passengers with a crew compliment of three hundred. The regular Carpenter had to rush ashore, owing to domestic trouble at home. However, the ship carried a Joiner and Carpenter's Yeoman. The Yeoman was to be my 'eyes' for the trip — a man called Crow. He was to be my shadow from the start. I was completely lost in the vastness and splendour of this magnificent twin screw ship, with a top speed of twenty five knots. After the little tramp steamer it was akin to sailing in a five-star hotel.

'Don't bother about a thing,' was the Foreman's advice. 'The Yeoman will show you the ropes.' My cabin was large and spacious. The sheer luxury of the cabin's interior left me spellbound.

Double bed, armchair and settee made up the lavish furnishing, and nestling on the bulkhead a telephone.

I'd no time to unpack — straight to stations, single up and let go. Orders didn't change. We were outward bound.

The Petty Officer's Mess was large and comfortable; white table-cloths, ye gods! And to make the perfect day, we PO's had access to the tourist class menu. I certainly wasn't used to this sort of VIP treatment. I just didn't know what hors d'oeuvres were, and when asked would I like an entree I said 'No, I'd like a nice steak'. It was cooked to perfection. The peach melba disappeared with equal relish.

The Crew Bar was known as 'The Pig and Whistle' where draught beer was on sale at a shilling a pint. A sailor strumming a guitar made the evening mellow and sanguine. 'The Porker' closed at ten-thirty, which was early for us dayworkers. I voiced my disappointment, only to be informed that The Stewards' Bar was open until eleven-thirty. The Stewards finished their duty rota much later than the dayworkers, hence the later opening time. I had another four or five pints before the shutter fell. It was time to zig-zag back to my cabin. I hadn't gone far before my unsteady progress was halted. A uniformed hand held me steady.

'Sorry Sir,' a voice said. 'Passengers are not allowed down here.' My eyes focused to make out a figure of an elderly man, the uniform was that worn by the Master of Arms (the Ship's Policeman).

'No passengers in the crew's quarters,' he insisted.

Knowing my working hours since signing Articles had been few was one thing, but to be called a passenger was somewhat of an insult. In a rather slurred and inebriated voice I said, 'I'm the Ship's Carpenter.'

'Yeah! And I'm fucking Billy The Kid,' he intoned without as much as a smile.

'Christ! What do I have to do to convince you?'

'Tell me you're not the Chippy for starters,' he grated, adding, 'you see, he happens to be a friend of mine. A drinking partner if you like.'

'That may be so, but the sad fact is he paid off just before we sailed. Domestic trouble and all that jazz.'

'First I've heard of it.'

'Well, you haven't heard that you're going to feel an idiot tomorrow either. But I can assure you here and now that you will; so be warned.' Just then another crew member staggered into view along the alleyway to substantiate my claim. The next morning at breakfast the Master of Arms apologised for his error, amid derisive smirks.

My main task on board centred on the fresh water tanks. With thirteen hundred people using them daily for personal hygiene and laundry, a twice daily check had to be carried out on the tanks.

The soup served at dinner had to be seen on an even keel. If it listed to one side of the plate it instigated enquiries into the ship's stability. The *Carenthia* had to be in the upright position for meals; this explained the presence of the telephone in my cabin. An hour before meals saw me busy with the Deputy Engineer below, transferring water from fore to aft and port to starboard. Going to sea could not be easier than this. In bad weather the enormous engines were 'shut in' and the giant stabilisers were unleashed to do their bit in steadying the steel monster.

The Carpenter's Yeoman, to his eternal credit, fetched me a silver tray each morning. Tea and toast in bed at six-thirty was somewhat of a novelty for Petty Officers. This voyage was to spoil me forever. Ships would never be the same again.

A considerable amount of time was spent on the maintenance of the electrically controlled fire doors and lifeboats. Strictly a grease-gun job. The Chippy's Yeoman ably assisted in this work. Another duty was to examine closely the Games Deck for splinters. Protruding heads of screws were another hazard, and on the priority list for neutralising. The Chief Officer warned of the occasional persistent passenger who wandered from deck to deck looking for these hazards. He or she would take advantage of them, using perhaps an old suit for the explicit purpose of suing the company for a new one. The mighty Cunard generally paid up, the case being considered too trivial and cheaper than a court action.

Montreal was a place where immigrants landed in the true sense of the word. The high and carefree voyage was over. The reality of life hit home as they were herded by Salvation Army personnel to various sidings for departure into the vastness of Canada's interior. Tears and tantrums were much in evidence as parents struggled with young children and lots of luggage. The Yeoman and I worked day and night to replenish the now depleted stock of fresh water. Our own watering hole was 'Smokey Joe's' waterfront bar. Beer at fifteen cents a glass enabled us to fill our tanks to a glowing and satisfying level. Yarns would be swapped and past trips re-lived as glasses moved up and down in a steady rhythm.

The homeward run was easier, only a few passengers to be molly-coddled. It was mind boggling to think that this whole process was repeated every thirteen days. I thought, rather selfishly, that I might be allowed to remain on this floating paradise. I didn't wish the other Carpenter any harm, just a broken leg or two.

Back ashore, in my little fender-making loft, things were not the same. A glimpse of life at sea on board a passenger liner left me with a longing for the briny and the wind-swept oceans, a feeling akin to being hooked on something — difficult to let go — the longing persists for another trip. Two years is about the limit. If you decide to get out and come ashore that's fine, but if not then a seaman becomes an object drawn and manoeuvred twixt moon and tide. Never settling and never ceasing to yearn for another voyage, knowing he is trapped but never admitting it. Floating like flotsam to lap against the jetty for a while before being drawn out again to ride the waves. A bottle with a message is what a seaman is. The former in his hand and the latter in his head.

During lunch hour, I quickly made up my mind to try another Company, this time though I wouldn't be hasty. Keeping my job in Cunard was of paramount importance. To secure another job first was the objective and so I soon found myself in another office. The shipping company was well-known. Yes, they wanted a Carpenter, the Deck Superintendent informed me. Was I willing to fly to the Middle East? Yes! I would be only too pleased to fly to the Middle East.

# Chapter 15

The flight, which would be my first, was scheduled to take off from the old London Airport. I travelled down to London by train and stayed overnight at the Merchant Navy Hotel for Officers at Lancaster Gate. I was still cutting near to the bone financially, and struggled by foot and bus with my gear to the airport.

My ticket was First Class on a BOAC Comet — the first jet airliner. It cost one hundred and thirty three pounds, which was about four months' wages for me then. All expenses were, of course, paid by the company. The flight was due to take off at one in the afternoon. I arrived at eleven, accompanied by a Quartermaster who was joining the same ship. He was a tall thin-faced character named Gary. His face was burned a dark tan from numerous voyages to the tropics. We were due to stop at Frankfurt and Istanbul and finally on to Basra in Iraq, our destination. I was elated to discover from a very friendly Steward that first-class passengers were entitled to free grog. This news was gratifying indeed. I had less than ten shillings in my pocket.

'Why are the other passengers drinking tea and coffee?' Gary queried, obviously thinking they were all insane.

'Because that is what they ordered,' the Steward said, flashing a smile.

We ordered large rums with a sense of urgency and greed, and were both well on our way to victory before touching down at Frankfurt.

The next stage of the flight was no less than a seven hour hop. We reached Istanbul in a warm and friendly glow. The rum by now had taken over. Some element or other had burned out in one of the engines, an item of information which was relayed to the passengers over the intercom. A delay was imminent. Who cared? I felt I could fly the rest of the way all on my ownsome!

We had to alight while repairs were hurriedly carried out. The passengers were enabled to get free refreshments in the airport terminal. By now Gary's previous trips had been re-lived and we vowed to be blood brothers for the duration. It was late that evening, towards midnight, before we were airborne for the final long haul to Basra. The lights were dimmed to enable the passengers to get some sleep.

The following morning, circling Basra, I awoke. It was seven-fifteen. I'd slept the whole night through and felt really chuffed. Gary, on the other hand, had spent a restless night. His false teeth were missing. The Steward was on his hands and knees, searching frantically under the seats for the molars. He eventually found them three rows astern. The lights warned us to fasten our safety-belts. We landed without any more fuss, but in those far off days of first-class travel the crew lined up by the exit to shake one's hand in a gesture of goodbye. I found this last act a little embarrassing, due, no doubt, to Gary's behaviour.

The month was August. The heat of the Persian Gulf was at its peak. The force of its intensity hit me as I disembarked. I'd heard tales of the Gulf and its indiscriminate glaring sun. The Abadan blues and various accompanying mental disorders were a matter of general knowledge and jargon amongst all seafarers. Hundreds of seamen of all nationalities had to cry-off annually from heat exhaustion. We were filling two such vacancies. It was only now that the shipping companies and federations were beginning to sit up and take notice. The older generation of seamen were the most vulnerable. Air conditioned ships had not yet arrived.

A shipping agent greeted us at the reception desk, we were bundled into a waiting taxi for a drive through the antediluvian streets of Basra. We arrived at the hotel. It immediately became apparent that our first-class status had ended. We were crew ... and as such, were installed in what could only be described as 'An Arab Hotel'. I will hasten to add that all hotels were Arab, but some were more modern than others. The one we were herded into was of the seedier kind. There was no glass in the windows, just timber shutters of the louvre type. A large slow-moving fan hung ominously from the ceiling. The beds were for folk more at home on a camel's back or more suitable for the shagging camel himself. Gary and I exchanged disapproving glances. It would only be for a couple of days, at least that is what we were told. Our ship was held up in another port, Bander Shapur. The couple of days turned out to be a whole month!

After the first day my body was covered in a very painful rash known as 'prickly heat'. This was sorely aggravated by the salt from body perspiration which flowed freely. A bottle of cold beer cost the equivalent of five shillings. The five Dinar advance which I subbed from the agent lasted two days. One Dinar was a Pound Sterling. The hotel food was without exception goat — goat's meat, goat's milk and goat's cheese. After a month of this, if anyone had shouted 'Billy' I would have responded automatically! We spent the several days examining the market area, watching the locals squatting around large hubbly bubbly pipes, each with his own stem, sucking away contentedly and dreaming of Allah's promised land.

The warm humid nights spent in the hotel bedroom were eerie. Lying naked on the bed had to be quickly discontinued when I discovered that the room was visited by large flying black beetles, known to seamen as 'Bombay Canaries'. These horrible airborne insects gave the unwary a nasty fright. Whether they gave you a bite or a sting is to pause and wonder, I don't know. They made my nights sleepless and anxious, that's for sure. Gary and I haunted the agent's office for news of our ship. Each day would bring a faint promise of another day, so it went on, until the agent, acting on orders from above, made plans for our journey overland to join the elusive ship.

I was still plagued with the scourge of prickly heat. A small boat ferried our party across the Shatt Al Arab, which divided Iraq and Iran. A Customs' checkpoint was the only sign that told us that the border was crossed. Persia, as it was formerly known looked no different from the side we had just left. Our documents were examined and entry visa duly stamped. A vast expanse of desert lay forebodingly ahead. A camel guide settled himself in the front seat of the taxi which had been hired to hurry us on our way. The windows of the cab were kept closed because of the clouds of dust which rose into the unbearable heat of the morning. It was a sauna bath on wheels streaking across the desert. Our destination was Abadan where we were due to stop for the night before travelling on to Bandar Shapur.

The track across was hard and lumpy. A dead Arab, lying prone, face upwards, was the only diversion. The taxi kept merrily on, he was beyond help. Another checkpoint, early in the afternoon, was our first stop. I'd removed my shirt and was sitting forward in the seat sweating freely, our thirst by now was acute. Our chatter, which had been easy and carefree at the beginning, now amounted to idle grunts and groans. Two bottles of coke each was our reward at this second stop. They were cold and delicious and revived our sagging morale.

After eight hours in this travelling hot box, we reached our goal. The Seamen's club in Abadan was residential and air conditioned, a welcome delight. It was like walking into an icebox from an oven; our rooms were similar. We decided unanimously to have an early night. It was to be the first completely restful night I'd had since arriving in the Gulf area. The following morning we were up and off on the final stage of our journey — this time by rail.

The train (if you could call it that) was windowless. The long wooden seats were shared with chickens, goats and Arabs. The latter were a good humoured lot and jabbered away sixteen to the dozen. Refreshments came by way of thin enamel beakers filled with milkless tea. Our fellow passengers were our benefactors. For this we were grateful, knowing in our hearts that they were in all probability poorer than we were.

There she was, our ship, lying shimmering in the middle of the Tigris. We finally climbed aboard with a great sense of relief. One journey was history, another lay in the optimistic future. The Chief Steward, I was to find out in the months that followed, was a kind and gentle man. In those days the Chief Steward was also the Medic. It was to him that steamy afternoon that my rash was shown and immediately diagnosed. Medicated soap was the prescribed cure, and it did in fact clear up the condition in days.

At last, our turn came to discharge cargo. The morale of the crew was at a low ebb from the prolonged wait. Gary and myself were the only two who showed any signs of contentment. Tropical hours were in force. We turned to at six in the morning and finished at midday. The sun was then at its peak and scorched all before it. I had an electric fan in my cabin which assisted in alleviating the discomfort from the heat. The soaring temperature was made worse by the engine room directly below the Petty Officer's living accommodation. Cold water, too, was a problem. No icewater tap on board. Buckets of water were deposited in the ship's fridge each morning and retrieved at lunchtime. Flasks were provided and filled. Four cans of cold beer were the daily ration, which helped.

I was to witness two incidents while the ship unloaded in Bandar Shapur. Both unrelated and both concerning Arabs. The first was a homosexual act between two men, who absolutely made no pretence of concealment or secrecy, indeed privacy. I, looking over a hatch coaming, purely out of curiosity, when movement below in the lower hold caught my eye. No, my eyes were not deceiving me. One Arab lay half sprawled across a large crate while another rhythmically seduced him. There were other dockers in the hatch, working away, apparently unperturbed at the sight in their midst. I was joined by another Petty Officer who exclaimed loudly, 'Some girls have all the luck, Chippy!'

The second incident occurred when a docker forced open a packing case. It contained a well-known brand of washing powder. The Arab was obviously unable to read English and foolishly thought it was food. The contents of the packet was disappearing down his throat at an alarming rate. I'd heard of the song 'I'm forever blowing bubbles', although I don't think it was written with washing suds in mind.

We sailed from the Gulf amid sighs of relief. The fresh breeze that blew on reaching the open sea cooled tempers as well as the ship. We were on our way to the Suez Canal, Quebec, Montreal,

New York, Baltimore and Philadelphia. Then on to the Panama Canal and America's West Coast, Los Angeles, San Francisco, across the North Pacific and the International Date Line to the Philippines, Manila, Hong Kong next, then Japan, Kobe, Nagoya, Shimazu, Yokohama through the inland sea then to Red China, Tsingtao and up the Yangesse to Shanghai, back to Singapore. Port Swettenham in Malay was next where Standing Orders decreed no unnecessary exposure on deck owing to the activities of Malayan Guerrillas who could fire at their leisure from the thick foliage on both banks of the river. The beautiful island of Penang was left in our wake with two of my teeth, extracted by a very proficient Chinese dentist. Columbo, now called Sri Lanka, was enjoyed before sailing homeward via Aden, Suez and London — Tilbury.

The time spent on Articles was ten months. The 'Mem Sahib's; in Japan were most memorable. Shimazu, nestling in the shadow of the sacred mountain of Fuijiama was, in my opinion, the highlight of the voyage. Singapore was where four of us hired a car to tour the island, taking in the infamous Changi-jail, a former Japanese prisoner-of-war camp, and the lines of white slabs marking the final resting places of allied soldiers, mostly Australian, at Krange War Cemetery.

I was loaded with presents from Japan. The rate of exchange then was a thousand yen to the pound. A set of China delf, consisting of twenty-four pieces, cost one pound. Everything was musical, jewel boxes and photo albums were purchased to bring home to family and friends.

Other interesting moments emerging from my frequent runs ashore occurred in Brooklyn when, in a state of alcoholic stupor, I mistakenly hailed a roving police patrol car for a taxi and tried to jump aboard only to be told firmly, 'Beat it limey!'

In Los Angeles I went on a spree with a Yankee sailor. He was only a rating, yet he persisted in telling me his father was a Southern plantation owner. He didn't have a Southern drawl, which in my reckoning, is synonymous with people born and reared in the Southern States. This fact I made known plainly and loudly. An argument followed which resulted in us both getting

the bums rush from the bar. That did not deter us. We simply
staggered off to the next neon sign, which said 'Bar', and continued with the discourse. He, with obvious bullshit, and me,
with equal helpings of blarney. Of course, his father had other
interests and I was invited to call at his lavish home next time I
was 'States-side'. I returned this offer of Southern hospitality
with an invitation of my own. By now it was clear that my father
owned half of Dublin City. I was the black sheep and, silly me,
had run off to sea.

In Shanghai, all hands had to assemble on deck while the
accommodation was searched. No cameras to be used either. The
run ashore was very good from our point of view. For instance, a
sewing machine could be purchased for as little as eleven
pounds. It was argued that the actual trip was a trip around the
world. Some said 'Out through the Suez and home via the
Panama constitutes circumnavigation of the globe'. I was one of
the other group who scoffed at such a suggestion. Why? Because
we hadn't crossed the Equator. All those countries we had called
at were in the Northern Hemisphere. In fact, the nearest we got to
the Equator was Singapore. The line is three degrees (or one hundred and eighty miles) south of the island.

Each morning and evening on board this vessel I would visit
the engine room, as part of my duty, for tank soundings. Shortly
after joining I became aware of the 'attentions' the Third
Engineer was paying me (especially ascending the ladder back to
the Main Deck). This young man would follow me closely. On
reaching the engine room entrance he would turn about and
descend again. This audacious behaviour continued for a couple
of weeks, much to my discomfort. It didn't go unnoticed among
the other crew members either, and a snigger here and a wink
there added fuel to my indignation.

Going to his cabin one day, I knocked on his door and angrily
demanded an explanation. He didn't seem surprised; in fact, I
could detect a slight smile on his face — he invited me in. Seeing
me hesitate, he hastened to say that he didn't want the whole ship
to know his business, indicating the officers' alleyway and
accommodation. I sat on the large settee, which took up the

whole after-end of his cabin. He then casually offered me a beer, which I accepted. He made himself comfortable in a swivel chair by his desk.

'You've guessed the truth I suppose?' he commenced.

'Yes, I have, and I don't like your advances. What's more, half of the crew are enjoying the show.'

;Yes, they don't miss much,' he said, adding 'I'm a homosexual and I've taken a fancy to you. I apologise if I've caused you any embarrassment; but while you're here,' he continued, 'I would still like to proposition you. We could make our meetings very discreet.'

'I'm not your man,' I said, rising to leave, 'and you're getting fair warning — don't follow me from the engine room again!'

'Fair do's, Chippy,' he whispered. 'But if you ever change your mind, don't hesitate to drop in.'

'I don't think there's any fear of that,' I said without malice.

Later in the voyage, southbound through Panama, I was relieved from my station on the f'c'sle head to have dinner. On entering my cabin to swallow a quick beer, before going to the Mess, I got a shock. Sitting in my cramped quarters was the Third Engineer. He appeared to be agitated, wild eyed and disturbed. I offered him a beer from my limited allowance. He declined.

'Is there something wrong?' I queried, feeling a little uneasy.

'They're all after me,' he said, sobbing.

'Who's after you? Tell me,' I probed. He named two of his fellow officers.

'One of them has an axe. They're going to kill me. Can I stay in your cabin, Chippy?' he pleaded.

'Sure you can,' I reassured him, soothingly. 'Stay as long as you like.' I left my cabin hurriedly. I'd lost all inclination to eat and made my way to the Chief Steward's quarters. He listened attentively while I related my encounter with the Engineer. He looked at me for a minute or two, twirling a pen in his fingers.

'Well Chippy,' he began, 'you realise the man is ill, don't you?' I nodded agreement.

'We have been watching him for some days now. His

behaviour has been odd, to say the least. Of course, if you want him removed from your quarters …'

'No,' I said hastily. 'I'll be on duty for some hours yet.' At Christoble that evening, the engineer, heavily sedated and encased in a strait jacket, was landed for hospitalisation. He was suffering a severe nervous breakdown.

My pay-off totalled one hundred and fifty-eight pounds. It was the most money I'd ever handled that I could really call my very own. I had presents for all the family. Plenty of clothes to wear and thirty-four days' leave. It was a great feeling having everything. I wanted for nothing and was really looking forward to going home. Reaching Euston I decided to travel home via Liverpool; look up some old shipmates, have a jar or two. Hell, life was good. No cares, no worries, no hassles.

I decided to treat myself to a sleeper and ordered tea and toast from the car attendant for the following morning. This was really the life. I slept soundly and awoke in a jubilant mood. I still had 'the channels', a condition known and reserved for all homeward bounders. I'd all day to get topped up in Liverpool. The Dublin ferry didn't sail till ten. The morning was 'blown' supping grog in Atlantic House. A couple of familiar faces and much shaking of hands followed by 'What's it going to be?'

# Chapter 16

Dublin, I'd arrived. The world was mine, king for a week, or near enough anyway. In ten days I was penniless, blew the lot. Santa Claus was an Irishman for sure. I still had my return ticket to Liverpool. My mother borrowed two pounds from a neighbour to tide me over., It all happened in an alcoholic haze. The North Wall loomed again, and the passenger boat back to Liverpool. I still hadn't learnt any lessons from previous spells of hardship. I wandered around Liverpool in a daze. My gear I'd left at the Mission. The Pool had nothing to offer either. A roof over my head was the priority. It was then the answer came, my salvation, yet again.

Working across the Mersey in Camel Laird's Dockyard were two young men. Men with whom I had served my apprenticeship back in Dublin. It was a long chance, but, at that particular time, no other options were available. Out of the throng of people that surged from the shipyard gate that evening I spotted Billy. He was surprised to see me, but also genuinely pleased. We swapped yarns about the missing years. At that time he was waiting to emigrate to Australia. My excuse for being down and out seemed rather feeble and pathetic in view of my recent extravagances.

Billy had a rented room and kitchen in Liverpool. I was welcome to share it, plus he parted with a few pounds! In all fairness I would have done the same for Bill, but, like other folk, we were unable to foretell the future and, alas, what the future had in store was grim.

I had by now become an established seaman which entitled me to a paltry weekly stipend of three pounds. One had to ship out rather quickly. I put in a request for my papers to be transferred from South Shields to Liverpool. This was accomplished without much ado but the manpower situation was causing concern. The root of the problem lay squarely at the door of the Ministry of Defence. The system then was two years' National Service or six years in the Merchant Navy. The seamen earned more money and generally had an easier time. With regular seamen the trouble was too many men for too few jobs. Trudging from one shipping office to the next was an everyday drudgery. Signing on at the Pool was necessary, or you would forfeit your three miserable pounds.

This bad spell lasted for weeks and Billy had more than his fill, struggling, as he was, to get some money together for his departure to pastures greener. I was contributing nothing to the housekeeping, and invariably lowered the boom on him particularly at weekends. The end came by way of a hint.

Each Friday evening I would meet Bill and we would get the groceries in for the weekend, at least he would, it was his money. One particular Friday my wait was in vain. No Billy. I sauntered to and fro for more than an hour after the usual time had come and gone. It had crossed my mind that he was working overtime or dropped off somewhere for a pint or two, but now seeing him framed in the doorway of his flat when I reached it, and reading the look on his face, it was painfully obvious that I had overstayed my welcome. It was a bitter pill to swallow, and yet, who could blame Bill? He had shared everything with me for weeks. There was never any intention of not repaying his kindness. It was simply a question of when! Finally, I went into the Pool and had a flaming row with the powers that be, saying in no uncertain terms that I was not prepared to spend my youth seeking a ship. They in turn, of course, pointed out that they could not give me what they didn't have. So another move was imminent. I vowed, yet again, that I would take greater care of my hard earned money on future trips.

I managed to get a travel warrant from the Seaman's Union. A five pound loan from yet another friend, and I was on my way to 'The Big Smoke'. I didn't see Billy again. He did get to Australia eventually, so did I, but I didn't know his address or even the area he settled in, but one thing is certain, I did try and haven't forgotten.

London loomed, the Pool was a busier shipping port than Liverpool; and I had to have a base and chose Kingston-on-Thames. Shipping was still going through a depression and jobs were scarce. My next ship came from an unexpected quarter. During my disastrous leave spent in Dublin I had, in a fleeting moment of sanity, called at the offices of Irish Shipping Ltd., and duly left my name and address. Now that I was residing in Kingston, Surrey, I wisely decided to drop a line to the shipping company informing them briefly of my altered circumstances. I had had to take lodgings and a job of work ashore. An income was a must. Each and every Saturday morning I travelled to Aldgate and the Dock Street Pool. Firstly to get a sea-going job, and second to visit some of the many friends I had who lived in the area. Then, when least expecting it, a telegram arrived from Irish Shipping offering a berth as carpenter on the *Irish Adler* lying at Tilbury.

The *Irish Adler* was a modern general cargo freighter on an Ellerman charter. It was to be my new home for almost twelve months, split into two voyages of five and a half months' duration. The *Adler* bunkered at Tenerife in the Canary Group before crossing the Equator in the South Atlantic, calling to discharge at Lobito in the Belgian Congo. We continued the voyage through to South Africa, calling at Capetown, Port Elizabeth, East London. Mauritius was next, a beautiful island in East Africa; then India — Calcutta, Pakistan, Chittagong and home via Trincomellee in Columbo, Aden, Suez Canal and finally Tilbury. After a short spell in Dublin on leave, we signed on again for another trip to the same ports.

The highlight of this trip was my arrest in Calcutta. I was ashore sampling the rum and coke, which, for reasons best known to the Indians, could be bought cheaper than beer. I was merry but not incapable when I hailed a rickshaw for the ride back to the ship. The night was warm and oppressive. The rickshaw wallah seemed tireless as he plodded through the dusty dockland streets. The sweet smell of decaying vegetables and gutter sewers added to the humidity. On reaching the dock gate I was assisted to the ground by an Indian who appeared to be there for no other purpose than to see that you got safely out of the rickety rickshaw hoping, no doubt, he would pick up a Rupee or two for his trouble. However, this particular wallah happened to be a pick-pocket, and, more to the point, an amateur. I say amateur simply because I caught him red-handed, actually with his hand in my pocket. Anyway, the Indians are among the finest pick-pockets in the world. More's the pity, this idiot I'd nabbed was not living up to standards. The money I had in my possession was less than five Rupees, equivalent to approximately forty pence. There happened to be a policeman on duty at the dock gate. It would be useless to clip this silly bugger on the ear and then attempt to stroll through the gate as if nothing had happened. The only alternative was to hand the pukla wallah (thief) over to the policeman. This move I was to regret because as it turned out the pick-pocket was in collusion with the pox of a bent policeman.

I tried, with various signs, to explain my predicament to the policeman. He quickly made it known that he wanted me to keep moving, saying something like 'Asti, Asti' and pointing in the direction of the berthed ships. The hair on my neck was beginning to stand on end. This bum was rubbing me up the wrong way.

'No Asti, Asti,' I growled, 'fucky fucky asti!'

All Indians know the spoken word 'fuck'. This thieving bastard of a copper was no exception. He was soon on the 'phone jabbering away in Bengali or some other native tongue. It wasn't long before an army-type truck hove into view. This was in service with the local 'bandits', for who, in their right mind, could call them 'policemen'?

Soon I was under arrest and on my way to Kiddipore Twenty Seven, the local nick. A doctor was summoned and asked me if I'd been drinking. I answered in the affirmative. He then pronounced me drunk. I was marched to a cell that could only be described as a cage. It was completely devoid of any sort of furnishings, three Indians squatted down in corners. The fourth corner was vacant. A channel cut through the centre of the cell carried running water and sewage. There was a guard with a Lee Enfield .303 rifle. He certainly wasn't used to handling it. This much I deduced from the awkward way he held it. I refused to enter the cell. I'd no desire to squat on a concrete floor and watch Portuguese Man-o-Wars bobbing through the sanitary water channel. The guard hesitated, looking back towards the station room where a Jamadar of officer rank was standing. After an anxious couple of moments, I was taken back to the comparative comfort of the station room, given a chair and there I remained until the following morning.

During the interim many prisoners were interrogated by the Jamadar. His method of persuasion was to use a broom handle across the back of the victim, who was first forced to kneel on his hands and knees. Whether this was to extract a confession from the unfortunate prisoner, or merely to implement punishment for a crime committed I'll never know, but I do know that the squeals of pain and pleas for mercy were frequent and urgent, and I am positive some of these people suffered permanent damage to their spine for life. I dozed fitfully in my chair and was relieved when the sun filtered through the louvres signalling the start of the day.

The wagon that called to take us to court reminded me of a circus animal conveyance. There must have been thirty of us crammed inside. All the prisoners' faces were pressed to the bars of this cage on wheels. Progress was slow. Teeming masses filled the pavements and streets. Taunts and jeers followed us along the route. The very fact that there was a white man among the forty thieves added to the interest shown by the general public. I heard the word 'Sahib' mentioned frequently. The court house could only be described as a horse pound. There were openings where the doors should be and the same applied to the windows. There were no chairs available. The only furniture was a large bench on which the judge rested his elbows. He didn't have a seat either. I don't know how or when my case was heard. I didn't even hear my name called. There was no interpreter or representative from the Company's agents or the ship. I was simply approached by a man who in limited English told me I had been fined sixty Rupees, which amounted to four pounds ten shillings Sterling. That sort of money I didn't have.

'Money on ship?' he asked.

'Yes,' I replied, 'plenty of money on ship.'

'We pay fine,' he croaked, 'you pay me on ship.'

I readily agreed to this amicable arrangement, but somehow felt that I was being taken for a ride. The case could have been dismissed if the truth was known, or at least a much lower fine imposed. This crafty individual was obviously a money shark who earned his living from the local courts. Paying peoples' fines who just happened to be down on their luck. He would then charge an exorbitant interest rate. Well, for the time being he suited my purpose. I wanted to get back aboard the ship.

It was close to midday before we left the court. The sun above was at its very peak and I sweated freely as I walked between this money shark and one of his henchmen. He looked at my face frequently as if trying to read my thoughts. I'd absolutely no intention of making a run for it. The main reason being I simply didn't know in which direction to bolt. This character was taking me sightseeing, deliberately. Anyway, to run would be foolish. Indians were prone to stoning wrong-doers. It only takes one to begin the hue and cry, before the rest of the populace join in the fun and stone you to death!

I eventually reached the ship and went straight to my cabin where I had some money. The money shark was warned to remain at the top of the gangway. A guard was posted there by courtesy of the agents. It was just a matter of ordering the guard to keep a weather eye on the pair of them, while I went to my cabin. I returned to the gangway within minutes and handed over a pound Sterling. The shark remonstrated loud and long, muttering dark threats. The guard, fearful of his job, then chased them along the wharf with a rather large and sturdy baton. The shark undoubtedly made a profit. The rate of exchange then was sixteen Rupees to the pound, but Sterling was also on the black market, fetching as much as thirty Rupees. The average docker's pay per day then was as little as two Rupees.

Of course, I had to explain my absence to the mate, who in turn informed the Old Man. The agent was duly brought into the verbal affray. At the end of the day it transpired that the practice of picking pockets, and police complicity, was widespread. So much then for India's 'independence'.

Many other interesting things happened on board the *Irish Adler* during my time on Articles, but they involve other seamen and, needless to say, that's their story.

'The older you get, the wiser you get,' the old saying does. I, naturally, wasn't the exception. Between ships, or jobs if you like, I would look in at the Pool, mainly to check if things were moving. If jobs were hard to get I'd simply take work ashore. My days on the beach were over. My base remained at Kingston, Surrey, and it still is to this very day. The girl I settled down with, although a native of Wales, had earlier sought employment in Kingston too. (For the record, we are still together.)

# Chapter 17

I was now back to unestablished status, after literally throwing my established contract at the official in the Liverpool Merchant Navy office. This act made future work scarce; all vacancies, naturally, going to the seamen holding a two year contract. To make matters worse, the big tanker companies such as Shell and British Petroleum were making the carpenter's rating redundant. This in turn was swelling the queue of those waiting to ship out. It was now only a question of sliding down.

In earlier days our biggest boost came from Lloyds who decreed that every ship of three thousand tons or over must carry a carpenter. When this clause was obliterated, it gave free reign to the shipping companies and they took full advantage of the act. It is sad because the shipwrights' trade was a noble trade and had been for hundreds of years. The carpenter was the top man on deck in days of sail and was addressed by the prefix 'Mister' by all crew members. When the world's oil supplies run dry, it is worth remembering that ships can still cross the vast oceans simply by returning to sail; although by then, the last shipwright will have long faded into obscurity.

At the time of writing there are about ten shipping companies left in the British fleet, whose ships still carry carpenters. But getting back to the earlier days, the jobs on offer to me were few and far apart, and those were only available in ships which other contracted chippies had refused, run jobs like taking a ship to the continent and back, or 'rocking', taking ships around the British coast, while the regular carpenter took his well-earned leave.

I was almost ten years at sea. the year was nineteen sixty-five, it was early December. The morning was chilly. I made my way to the Pool. I'd just taken a ship called the *Harpagus* from Rotterdam to Glasgow and earned for myself twenty-four hours leave. The old Shipping Federation building in Dock Street had closed and a new and modern building in Prescott Street was now open for business. Its proximity was in fact only two or three hundred yards from the old Pool. I pushed my book across the counter fully expecting a blank. Much to my surprise the official said, 'There's another one in Rotterdam going deep sea,' and went on to add, 'would you like it?'

'Where is she bound for?' I asked.

'Haven't a clue,' he replied. 'The information I have is, you stay at The Red Ensign Club tonight. A coach will pick you up at eight-thirty tomorrow morning and take you to Folkestone; there you catch the ferry. Another coach will be waiting at the Hook of Holland to take you to the ship.

'What Company?' I asked. This was always a clue to the run.

'Haine Norse Management, the m/v *Tremeadow*.' I knew instantly it was a tramp. A name given to ships with no regular run. Furthermore, they had lost a ship carrying grain in the North Atlantic some years earlier when her cargo of grain had shifted in a storm, the *Tresillan*. She sank with some loss of life.

'She'll do,' I said.

That evening, in The Red Ensign Club, I encountered some of the other crew members. And speculated on the port of call and on the duration of the trip. There were many and varied guesses and all in good humoured banter and, of course, all wrong.

We arrived safe and sound the following evening. Spirits were high. The accommodation was midships with my cabin situated on the after end on the port side, adjacent to the Crew's Mess. Depositing my gear on top of the bunk I immediately made my way forward to the Officer's Quarters, to introduce myself to the Mate. He was a very tall Yorkshire man, and for the duration of the voyage turned out to be as good as the best. But now he was non-committal.

'We're getting our Orders in the Channel,' he said, in answer to my anxious query.

Orders in the Channel were always a bad omen; but more to

the point, the Old Man and the Mate invariably knew the Company's Orders. It was simply a question of discretion, to stave off the inevitable stampede and mass desertion by the crew if the truth were leaked. When the blow came it was a hammer blow. Steaming, as you were, down the Channel, outward bound. The Orders were received in numb silence. Out of all the guesses from all the know-alls, none could have imagined or dreamt in their wildest dreams our destination.

'Proceed to Buenos Aires to load grain for Communist China' and still in the dark as to where we were bound from there.

The foul language that whistled across the Channel from the fore deck of the *Tremeadow* would surely make the white cliffs of Dover blush. The news was even less heartening for me because although never frightened of work, this would be toil beyond compare. Shifting boards and feeders would have to be located and dragged from murky corners of hatches. It was also quickly established from the ship's log book that the *Tremeadow* hadn't carried grain for eight years.

The expected run to Buenos Aires was fourteen days. Compulsory overtime was introduced, all hands on day work. This ship, it transpired, was equipped with an iron mike, an automatic pilot. All hands were to be called at five-thirty in the morning, ready to commence work at six. The day's work would end at ten. A shower, followed by a cup of tea and into the bunk by eleven. Well it had to be done and we succeeded. Sailing up the River Plate, we paused to gaze at the protruding mast of the *Graf Spee*, a German warship lying peacefully in her grave since World War II. We were just putting the finishing touches to number five hatch. All hands were looking forward to drawing a sub on their wages and a good run ashore. Well, I can honestly say none was disappointed.

We sailed, loaded to the Plimsoll, for China. It was well into the third week of January with Orders to bunker at Durban and Hong Kong. Of course, bunkering ports means just that. There is no shore leave and the average stay in Port is twelve hours or so. In transit, we had all the other work to bring up-to-date. All the general maintenance work that had been neglected preparing for the shipment of grain. But now the pressure was off. All hands were turning to at seven in the morning and working until eight at night.

Not so many days out from Buenos Aires, the *Tremeadow's* engine began to give trouble. Finally we stopped. Emergency repairs were instigated. In the meantime we wallowed like a cork in the briny. A ship without power rolls violently in the mildest of seas. After eight hours or so we got underway again. The failure of the engines took on a pattern. That is to say we broke down frequently, on one occasion for almost twenty hours, and there's nothing so boring as going nowhere. In crew jargon the name of the ship changed constantly from *Tremeadow*, to Tresnail, then Trecreeper, Trecrawler, Trestopper and finally Trefucker. To top it all the Chinese authorities kept us guessing as to our port of call. Finally we received orders to drop anchor. The port was in North China. It was bitterly cold, the month was March; the spray whipping over the side was freezing to the deck. Morale was low, knowing there would be no fraternisation with the local beauties, and still in limbo regarding our next cargo. Would we be homeward bound or not?

When we did eventually get alongside, the Old Man decided one advance on wages and one only. As this was a remote part of China and a first visit to the port of Ching Wang Tao, we were naturally cautious as to the amount drawn. My own sub was a mere twenty-five pounds or the equivalent in 'Yuon', the Chinese currency. This was a mistake which I will always regret if I live to be a thousand and two!

The first surprise of the evening was the taxi. I climbed inside at the dock gates. It just drove away before I'd time to utter a word. All effort to make conversation was ignored completely. When it finally came to a halt I found myself at a very spacious and modern Seamen's Club. The taxi driver refused all attempts at remuneration.

When I entered the Club the cab fare was requested by one of the many staff. They all spoke excellent English. The actual charge was a matter of pennies. Steak, egg and chips was just one of the many European dishes to be had on the menu, besides their own excellent cuisine. Beer, by the bottle, which really had a kick in it, cost tenpence (and I mean old pence). Vintage Champagne could be bought for fifteen shillings a magnum!

After a couple of blissful evenings spent at this marvellous Club it was time to buy a few presents from the curio shop before all my money went on grog. My first purchase was a camphor chest, plus a few other small items. While browsing around this larger than large shop I happened on a pair of vases and naturally queried their age, etc., only to be told, in a matter-of-fact way, by a matter-of-fact assistant that they were four hundred years old and they cost a miserable twenty-five pounds!

As the port was only about fifty miles from the first gateway of the Great Wall of China we naturally asked and received permission to pay it a visit. A mini bus was duly supplied by the authorities. Much to my surprise, only ten of the crew accepted the offer. We were allowed a half day by the Old Man. No cameras were allowed, but we could buy photographs of the scene in a small shop close to the Wall. I remember vividly, while the bus was stopped at a road junction, how a young Chinese kid — perhaps five or six years old — stared in open-mouthed and wide-eyed wonder at the spectacle before him. It was obviously the first time he had seen a white man. I put on the ugliest face I could (which on reflection wasn't difficult) and glared through the window at the youngster. With a mighty yelp he turned and fled. No doubt in the direction of home and mother.

The Great Wall is approximately two thousand miles long. It has ten gateways at regular intervals. It is the wonder of all wonders; and is the only man-made object that can be seen from outer space. It goes up mountains and down valleys, in mind-boggling fashion, it is symmetrical throughout. There is room on top for two cars to pass each other with ease. The bricks are man-made and are the colour of coal slag and, indeed, could possibly be made from such a substance. The approximate measurement is twelve inches by six inches by four inches. Standing on top of the wall one could look down into Mongolia. Small kilns in sight of each other, filled with dry tinder, ready to be set ablaze when any particular part was vulnerable and likely to be attacked, was the method of communication.

About an hour before we sailed, a large black limousine drove along the jetty and stopped at the gangway. What we deemed to be an important official alighted. He was carrying an open black velvet tray with many and varied pieces of jewellery. He was accompanied by another man. Both went straight to the Old Man's quarters and invited him to take his pick. He chose a pair of ear-rings, no doubt with his wife in mind. Their value? One could only guess.

Being a warm weather sailor I was glad to leave the ice cold waters of China astern. At last we knew our fate — Bangkok — to load tapioca for Bremen, Germany. Thailand was tropical which suited me fine. Ah, it was nice to get the shirt off and tackle the many jobs on deck which had been botched during the cold spell.

With the war in Vietnam in full swing it was reasonable to expect a little close attention from the American airforce which flew low overhead. Call it buzzing if you like, the Navy of the Us shadowed us too. Our red-duster had to be kept flying from dawn to dusk. Most ships that visit Bangkok have to moor at buoys in the middle of the river. The river, of course, is like a freeway, with floating shops sailing up and down selling their wares, anything from a meal to the favours of a young girl.

Now, if you happen to be a crew member of a ship in the Tropics and the said ship does not have an ice-water tap, it is difficult to satisfy your thirst, because the warmth of the sea temperature will effectively have made the ship's drinking water in the double bottoms tepid. This then was our lot on the *Tremeadow*, when one's ration of four cold beers was expended. So you can imagine the absolute delight of all hands when one of the many floating shops tied up at our gangway. Case after case of ice-cold beer was carried on board and stowed under an awning. The crates were surrounded by ice-bags before being put on sale. Word soon got round that there was lots and lots of ice-cold grog to be had. Most of the deck hands were soon gathered at this oasis, licking their lips. The subs (or advance on wages) had not been issued, in fact the ship had only docked that self same morning. This was somehow conveyed by signs and pidgin English to the Thailander. He seemed to understand, and understand much too quickly for my liking. He smiled with beneficence and said, 'Sign, please, sign. No money. Sign please,' flashing another smile and a note-book. One crew member stepped smartly forward and plucked a cardboard crate containing twelve large bottles of beer. He signed his name, 'Mr Mickey Mouse'. This act did not go unnoticed by the others, who now wanted to know what it tasted like.

'Great swag,' was the burping sailor's verdict amid gales of laughter.

Soon Mr Donald Duck was in for a crate, so was Mr Yogi Bear, not to mention Mr Fred Flintstone, Brer Rabbit, and a host of other crazy names. Not all of the crew were tempted, but I do know that more than one Officer signed fictitious names. I abstained for reasons stated. Needless to say Mickey Mouse and Donald Duck and all the other comedians got happily blotto daily. Ten days elapsed before we were loaded and battened down, awaiting the Pilot, and Customs clearance to slip our moorings.

The Thailander, who had steadfastly brought fresh supplies each day, had cleared away his surplus grog from the deck, but his boat was still tied to the gangway; he himself was still on board.

The Police and Customs duly arrived. Permission to sail was refused. Reason being the publican hadn't been paid. The Old Man was furious. All hands had to line up on deck. The Thailander tapped each of his customers on the shoulders saying — 'Mr Mickey Mouse him,' and showed the sum outstanding to the Agent and the Policeman. Of course, each individual had to own up. It was their handwriting anyway; but what really hurt was the amount they were charged. One member of the catering staff had to pay forty-five pounds, which was almost a month's wages. If the truth were known, the real value of the beer was probably less than ten pounds.

Another eerie thing, worthy of mentioning here, happened on

the homeward run via Aden. A foul smell developed in the Officers' dining saloon. It was situated on the Bridge Front, spanning the breadth of the ship from port to starboard, and directly below the Old Man's Quarters. The Bridge Front was solid riveted steel. The Main Deck too was obvious solid steel and the interior of the saloon was, needless to say, highly polished mahogany panelling. The Bridge Front was watertight, the panelling, intact with battens to cover the joints, appeared untouched, so what was causing the smell and where was it coming from?

The stench became unbearable. Indeed, the saloon became uninhabitable. I was finally brought in on the act and ordered to find the source. I had to wear a mask. I gently removed the battens, to avoid scratching the polished veneer, and began unscrewing the panels. After the first panel was eased free the smell intensified. All was revealed behind the second panel. The source of the offending 'pong' was none other than the badly decomposed carcass of one very large rat; but to add to the mystery — and mystery it was — I also discovered six transistor radios, plus one empty beer carton. The possibility of the horrible smell being the result of the dead rat had of course been considered, but a thorough search of the saloon had failed to show any signs of entry, and, more to the point, had there been a way in for the rat he would surely have found his way out by the same means. No, this rat had died of thirst and hunger, no doubt having slipped behind the panelling when it was removed to conceal the radios, its escape route effectively blocked when the panel was resited. The cardboard beer carton gave the only clue, in conjunction with the ship's log book. The transistors, which were small, were undoubtedly placed in the carton before being concealed. The rat had nibbled away at the cardboard in an effort to stave off hunger. The name of the beer, which was clearly distinguishable, was American from the Great Lakes region. The *Tremeadow*'s log showed that the area had not been visited since nineteen fifty-seven, so our little haul had lain there concealed for a period of nine years. Had the rat been there all that time? In those days, small transistors were not as plentiful or as easy to purchase as they are today, so it is reasonable to assume that they would have been worth a fair amount of money, but why choose the Officers' Dining Saloon, which is in use from morning until night, and any hammering or noisy disturbance would be clearly heard by the Old Man whose living accommodation was directly above? Certainly no previous ship's Carpenter would in his right mind have adopted such a spot for smuggling when he would have easy access to other less conspicuous and more favourable parts of the ship. One other thought comes to mind. In my experience on ships, the Officers' Saloon is locked each evening after dinner. The Second Steward would be in possession of the key, so too would the Purser and the Mate, but — oh dear, groan, and shagging groan — that rat must have been the most unfortunate rat that ever lived; for happening on the most idiotic would-be smuggler that the British Merchant Navy establishment has ever sent Deep Sea.

To keep the radios on board meant that their presence would have to be declared on the manifest and of course their source, which would, in turn, give the Customs scrummagers a field day tearing the ship apart; so the Captain decreed (and rightly so, in my opinion) that they be given a watery grave along with the rat. These instructions were carried out post-haste and not without a fair share of grumbling from others who would have liked to keep at least one of the radios.

The *Tremeadow* was still having engine trouble; and while the ship wallowed in the briny, we endeavoured to keep balance. But spare a thought for our predecessors. The men who put to sea under sail and would, during any normal trip, lie becalmed for days on end. Why should we complain?

# Chapter 18

We reached Bremenhaven, the voyage had lasted just under six months. Much to our delight, there was to be a general pay-off. This was a relief to us all because the longest seamen's strike in history was looming and all hands were apprehensive, fully expecting to be retained on Articles. Well, we worried unduly. We paid off and were cruising in a luxury coach to Amsterdam Airport as drunk as drunk could be; there to catch a plane for Heathrow. Things got a little tricky when the driver of the coach refused to stop to enable all and sundry to empty their bladders. a near mutiny ensued before the driver capitulated under threat of physical violence. He stopped and soon clouds of steam could be seen drifting across the Autobahn. The German driver sat muttering protests in his native language, undoubtedly concerned about his licence. I arrived home three days before the strike commenced; I had lost forty-nine pounds in weight. Fourteen and a half stone when I signed on, and eleven stone when I signed off. For a six footer I looked a shadow of my former self.

The strike lasted approximately eight weeks. Luckily for us, we had almost a month's leave with pay. The remaining weeks saw me working as as general labourer on a building site. This was a complete change and contrast, and just what was needed. I was still ploughing through my accumulated earnings. The weekly three pounds strike pay would have just about put me back in my former residence — 'Skid Row'.

The strike ended with the seamen no better off financially; the damage to the economy was astronomical and the Merchant Navy became the last section of the British Industry still working overtime for single pay. The establishment lost most of its first-class seamen. Sailors, who like myself had taken jobs ashore for the duration, were now reluctant to surrender their new found security for the rigors and uncertainties of sea-going life. The Labour Government of the period demanded higher productivity. A question I felt like asking was, 'What can a seaman produce?' The end product was that the number of seamen who manned conventional ships was reduced, thus adding to the already alarming accident statistics. Of course, later, more modern ships didn't need as many men, but conventional ships continued to require the numbers set down by the Board of Trade. However, unlike a lot of others, I got back to sea and many and varied were the companies as ships came and went.

In my wake were many ports, some visited again and again. The Bermuda Triangle was crossed and re-crossed, an area which I found mostly mild and calm, the later controversy which surrounded this part of the world and captured the interest of many, left me rather bemused, but if I had to throw my weight behind any single theory, it would be that the area is prone to underwater earthquakes.

Vancouver, Los Angeles, San Francisco, Honolulu, and the Fiji Islands (Suva) were visited. Honduras, Texas, the Mississippi and Panama. Israel, the Lebanon, Turkey, Cyprus, Malta, Algiers, the Greek Islands such as Patras, Gulf of Corinth, Italy, Sicily, Gibraltar, Spain, Portugal, Sweden, Denmark, Norway and Finland. In fact, there was almost nowhere on earth I hadn't been ashore except Australia and New Zealand.

It was now 1969 and in my estimation time to tuck these two runs ashore under my belt. To do this, all one had to do was choose a company who made regular runs down-under, such as P&O Lines, New Zealand Shipping, Port Line, and the large Blue Star Line. These latter two had merged to become one of the biggest South-bound fleets at sea. All their ships carried carpenters and although they had many old ships afloat, they were happy ships. The average round trip to the Antipodes was six months, made up of six weeks outward bound, six weeks discharging, six weeks loading and the run for home, a further six weeks. The rather long periods taken to load and discharge arose because one dealt with mostly part cargo for many and varied ports, such as Freemantle, Adelaide, Melbourne, Sydney, Brisbane, Hobart and Tasmania. Across to Kiwi to load for home. North and South Islands included Wellington, Napier, Hamilton, Nelson and Bluff, the latter named was supposed to harbour the last pub before one set out for the South Pole! However, I believe there is another 'watering hole' a little further South on Steward Island. Other ports in New Zealand were, of course, Auckland, Wangerie, Port Chalmers and Dunedin. The entrance to Sydney Harbour and Port Chalmers I believe to be the most scenic on earth.

I chose Blue Star Line in my quest for work, assuming my chances of employment would be greater. My hunch proved correct. I knew Port Line had a small crew office in the Royal Albert Dock, and it was here I went, armed with the necessary identity card and discharge book. I was still short of money and always seemed to leave finding work until my last pound or two hove into sight. Today was no exception, but by now I had lots of sea-going experience and all my discharges with the exception of the earlier VNC, were very good. Both for conduct and ability. After examining my book, the shore-based foreman asked if I would be interested in taking a ship called the *Port Lincoln* coast-wise from London to Liverpool. This offer was a start with the company, so I obviously said yes.

We arrived outside the locks on the Mersey at five in the evening and although all hands were aware that the river tugs were on strike, we still expected to be tied up alongside with ample time to get ashore. Seven hours later, we were stood down from stations. It was past midnight, the language was foul even by seamen's standards, and it would have taken a brave man to admit he was a crew member of a tugboat. These coastal jobs, as they were widely known, were given to non-employees whenever possible, invariably to test their quality as seamen, and I'd be the last person to put my name forward as a candidate for perfect seaman. I would say, however, in all honesty that I never shirked work, in fact, I thrived on it. I was sacked on a couple of occasions but it was certainly never for laziness.

I was immediately offered another ship with the Blue Star Line. This one, I was told sombrely, would be Deep Sea, sailing from Liverpool via the Cape of Good Hope for the Australian coast, and all the ports I have just mentioned; it was to be only one of many such trips I'd make to the other end of the earth and the beginning of many happy years spent with Blue Star Line. It would also bring to an end almost a lifetime spent riding the waves. My first Blue Star ship, the *Royal Star*, had been bombed during the War, off Algiers, with the loss of two men. She was enjoying a new lease of life.

It was early on a Sunday evening when I emerged from Lime Street Station still humping my toolbox around as part of my personal belongings. It was early enough to enable me to deposit my gear on board and still have time to get back ashore for a few pints of grog. Life was sweet, I reasoned, settling back comfortably in the cab which was taking me past some very dear and familiar landmarks. The taxi driver dropped me almost at the gangway. It didn't take much figuring out which to take aboard first, my suitcase or my toolbox. No one in their right mind would attempt to heave my toolbox away on their toes!

I had to go and announce my arrival to the Mate and collect the keys to my cabin and workshop. My cabin was small and situated on the After End. Cabins, of course, are basically for sleeping in and stowing one's gear. More time is spent working on deck and although it would be home for the following six months or so, I was not unduly worried. Actually, the voyage lasted five months and twenty-five days.

Having dumped my case on the bunk, it only remained to retrieve my toolbox from the quay. This July Sunday evening was warm and tranquil. The giant jibs of the cranes lay idle. A fluttering of foraging pigeons and a squawking of gulls were the only sounds, apart from the sound of my own foot-steps on the steel deck. Suddenly, a cabin door crashed open and out into view stepped a crew member. He was stark naked, sober and holding his cory in both hands.

'Can you beat this one for size? he demanded.

Apart from his sudden appearance which gave me an initial

shock, the weapon he held aloft was equally shocking.

'Mine couldn't beat the hairs on that,' I reassured him hastily.

Anyway, it was reassurance he wanted. He was on an ego trip. He insisted that I should flash mine and I was equally determined to keep it concealed.

'If all hands turned to and put their dicks end to end, you would still win,' I reassured him. These words seemed to appease him. Cackling wildly he returned to his cabin, slamming the door as he did so. I retrieved my toolbox and put it in my cabin before going ashore for a last fling.

I found the Australians very down to earth, forthright and likeable. It is a marvellous, wide, vast and warm country and the number of seamen who jumped ship (or 'skinned out') was numerous. It became an offence later to do this, and much more difficult. It carried a prison sentence too before a deportation order was implemented. It was rumoured that a bounty would be paid to informants giving the whereabouts of deserters. Girls, it was said, enticed men to miss the ship only to turn them over to the immigration authorities when the vessel had sailed. I never found any evidence to substantiate this claim, but then no girl ever asked me to stay. I'll assume that they were glad to see my departure.

On returning to London, we were given the usual going over by the Customs. In the steering flat they discovered a rifle. The troubles in Ireland were gathering momentum so it was natural I suppose for the Irish crew members to be the first to come under suspicion. I being one of four such men was ushered out on deck.

My only gripe was that I had had a very hard day and a painfully long stint at stations during the evening. It was gone one in the morning before the order to 'Stand down' was given, so needless to say I was showered and in my bunk almost immediately. Within an hour I was hauled out on deck while my cabin was searched and all my personal letters read, in an effort to establish some connection with the IRA.

We paid off later that morning, but then, after visiting such wonderful ports, there was the usual problem of not enough money to last out one's leave. Three months on the Australian and New Zealand coast had exhausted my earnings.

Into the seventies, conditions changed rapidly for British seafarers. Voyages were on average four months duration. This was good for morale. Accommodation too had improved rapidly, giving seamen their own single berth cabins, complete with shower and toilet. This transformation didn't happen overnight. Naturally, it was phasing out of the old and a gradual introduction of the new, thus enabling the fleet to become streamlined and competitive.

The carpenter's position on board ship was progressively sacrificed. Super tankers were putting to sea with less men than small conventional ships. Suddenly, men were being paid off at the nearest convenient port, It could be Sydney, Vancouver — it didn't matter; fly here, fly there. I was beginning to think I was in the Airforce! But reason prevailed through all this hustle and bustle. I'd been at sea too many years not to have learned a trick or two. What I needed was as regular runner and Blue Star provided just that.

The ship was the *Buenos Aires Star*, sailing from Victoria Dock London to Santos and Rio de Janiero in Brazil, to Montevideo in Uraguay and, of course Buenos Aires in the Argentine. The round trip was on average eight weeks, with an approximate ten days in London. Who could ask for better? Certainly not I.

Having passed the Canaries outward bound, we could normally bank on good weather and usually got it. Having sailed safely through many years of injury-free voyages and being acutely aware of the dangers and risks involved, it was reasonable to assume that sooner or later I would become a number in the rather alarming high statistical rate of injuries which were the seaman's lot; the accident rate, being the highest throughout the British industrial scene. Yes, even higher than the mining and building industry, and thanks to productivity deals resulting from the strike, the rate was climbing.

I witnessed one man, his finger almost severed at the first joint, simply bite it off, spit it contemptuously over the side and continue working. He uttered only two words, as part of his finger hit the sea — 'Fuck it!'

This particular voyage, like many others which preceded it, was no different in any shape or form. The ship was battened down and made ready for sea. We were assisted by two tugs through the locks and accompanied for a short distance down the Thames. The lines were cast off and we were on our own.

Gale warnings were forecast for most areas, including Dover, the Channel, Biscay and Finnistere. All in our path, but nothing new to us except that it would probably slow us down and perhaps add a day or two to the duration of the voyage. We caught the full force of the gale in the Bay of Biscay. That stretch of water which we normally crossed in sixteen hours actually took us four days. It transpired that another British ship, namely the *Eagle*, carrying passengers and cars, was also caught in this storm. Some of the passengers suffered broken limbs and subsequently sued for damages. The case went to the Old Bailey some years later, where a QC for the plaintiff described the storm as 'the worst in living memory'. Well, who am I to argue with a QC?

At the tail end of the storm, I received some caustic burns. I was using caustic soda to clear a blocked pipe in the fridge flat, when the ship took a sudden lurch into a trough, sending the caustic soda in all directions. I was wearing a boiler suit which absorbed the bulk of this horrible liquid; however, a minute drop entered my eye. Some had also got onto my foot, but I didn't feel the discomfort in that region of my body, due to the excruciating pain in my eye. It really felt as if a lighted cigarette had been stubbed out in my eye. I could feel myself passing out, but somehow managed to fight off the nausea. I knew also that I would have to reach cold fresh water to flush my eye, and quickly. Every second counted. The nearest fresh water tap was in the Stewards' shower on the next deck. There was no other crew member in the vicinity as I stumbled and groped my way along the alleyway. The ladder, the water, salvation — or so I thought — was only a matter of minutes away, but nevertheless it was minutes too late. The damage was done.

The ship immediately altered course for Lisbon. My eye ball turned black and already green puss was running down my face.

The Mate, to his credit, kept pumping morphia tablets into me, but nothing it seemed would stop the waves of pain that engulfed me. Words could not describe the horror of it all. A gigantic nightmare with a tormentor jabbing away with a red hot poker. When would it end?

We were eighteen hours steaming for Lisbon. Friday morning gave way to Friday evening. Friday night the agony continued. Saturday seemed a galaxy away, but slowly the painful hours slipped by. Friday night was spent twisting and turning in writing moments of relief-seeking positions. I didn't think of my eye any more. Just take away the pain!

Saturday morning we anchored off Lisbon. A launch was waiting to run me ashore. I was helped onto the liberty boat, which soon gathered speed for shore. The outline of the ship receded as we approached the quay. Willing hands assisted my climb to the jetty. An ambulance wailed its mournful way to hospital and there, for the first time in almost twenty hours, relief from pain. Drops into my eye effectively froze it. The sigh I'm sure was audible for miles around and sleep inevitable and welcome.

The British Hospital, Lisbon, is a private affair, and maintained financially by wealthy British patrons who have settled in Portugal for health and tax reasons. The Raj is nearer to home, so it seems.

Here the sight of my eye was saved and nursed back to health in just under three weeks. After the first few days in hospital, it became painfully clear that I would have to have a skin graft on my foot. It could not be done in Lisbon because the operating theatre was closing down for renovation. Queen Mary's, Roehampton, South West London was my next port of call and after a further three weeks of tender care I was 'ship-shape' again.

My position on board the *Buenos Aires Star* was secure. The ship would be back the following week, but in the meantime, a visit to the local Social Security Office was necessary, indeed pressing. After all, it was industrial injuries' benefit. The official listened to my legitimate claim and then disappeared into an inner office. He re-emerged minutes later to give me some sombre information.

'Sorry, we do not deal with seamen's claims here.'

'Oh! And where should I go then?'

'Newcastle on Tyne deals with seamen's claims, sorry.' And so say all of us.

Later on, I sought legal advice in an endeavour to obtain compensation, at a cost of twenty-five pounds. A QC advised me against claiming damages.

'A storm,' he said, with an air of finality, 'is an Act of God.' So now we all know! But I'll add this, God has a lot to answer for, and if He's about when I arrive, I'll punch Him straight on the nose!

# Chapter 19

It was nice to get back to sea and feel the cool breeze of a South Atlantic evening easing the humidity of one's cabin. I'd completed another voyage since leaving hospital. This would be my second.

As we approached the South American coast I was busy working in the lower hold of number two hatch, unable to avail myself of the continuous sunshine that one would normally enjoy working on deck. We arrived off Rio de Janiero and went to anchor. There was no berth available. The anchorage at Rio de Janiero lies about eight miles off shore. It isn't popular with seamen because the jolly boats are few and far between. Invariably one would call at the gangway midday, six and midnight. To miss the boat back spelt disaster. Most seamen preferred to wait 'til the ship tied up alongside when one could come and go as one pleased.

Sunday was overtime. The work in the hatch continued. Shortly after lunch I felt distinctly unwell. Every single piece of timber I cut was cut after a pause for breath. It was an effort to drive home the nails. Finally, I had to call a halt and make my way from the lower hold to the main deck. It was a vertical ladder and the climb sapped by remaining strength. Several stops on the way aloft, and fear lest I would pass out, didn't help.

When I reached the accommodation I was the colour of chalk. Fortunately, my distress didn't go unnoticed. Another crew member was at my side, assisting me to my cabin and my bunk. Yes, he did ask the classic question: 'Are you all right Chippy?'

No! Needless to say, Chippy was not all right. In fact, I was ill with 'El Grippe', but at that moment in time I'd never even heard of 'El Grippe'. My first attack came as the crew member disappeared in search of the Mate. I lay prone on my bunk, a tingling sensation began at my toes and worked quickly up through my body, to hold me paralysed for perhaps half a minute. The only parts of my body moveable were my eyelids. It was a terrifying experience. I felt unbelievable heat and exhaustion. The Mate appeared, but what could he do, except tell me to rest. Two days later El Grippe was diagnosed, it means 'The Grip' in Spanish. The next day I was sent to see a doctor. The doctors were having a hard time of it. Two doctors were employed by the Agents to care for all seamen who entered the port of Rio, as luck would have it. A German and a Greek seaman had to be operated on that very same day for appendicitis.

The surgery was full of seamen. Men of various nationalities. No other English-speaking sailors were present. I felt desperately ill and regretted obeying the order to 'Go ashore'. The Doctor arrived obviously harassed and upset. It was almost six in the evening, I'd been waiting four hours. My turn came for examination. He checked my blood pressure and said in his limited English, 'Very high. Very high.'

He continued saying this parrot-fashion, and heaped box after box of tablets onto my outstretched hand. (Actually five in all.) I left the surgery in a daze; too ill to be angry and acutely aware that I'd missed the jolly boat. I reached the jetty in a state of utter despair.

Brazillians speak mainly Portuguese and their currency is Crezeiros. In my pocket was a solitary five pound note sterling. I tried bribing the boatmen — any of them — to take me out to the ship, offering the five pound note as an incentive. This was steadfastly refused by one and all, each indicating that he wanted ten. The main problem was my condition, for if I was to pass out now I would simply be picked up by the police and treated as a drunken seaman and be thrown, unceremoniously, into one of their hell holes, known as cells. I knew some of the crew would be ashore. My only chance was to find one of them and put my very vulnerable self in their care. There were literally dozens of bars in the dock area, all busy and noisy. Every bar I entered girls approached and propositioned me. Some very nice girls too, but I could barely stand and they expected to be screwed.

'No palata,' I would say. A few disgusted looks came my way, but they didn't linger. 'No palata' is South American Spanish for 'No money'. All the girls knew that bit. I was almost out on my feet, going from bar to bar. Not a friendly face in sight, when suddenly my name was being called. 'Chippy! Chippy!'

My eyes searched frantically for the source. Was I delirious? No I wasn't. There they were. Two crew members on the other side of the road. Saved! I remained with them until the jolly boat departed for the ship at eleven-thirty. I returned to my bunk, vowing to die there or be cured. I knew it was more than blood pressure, but what? Immediately another attack of El Grippe seized my body. I really felt as though I was going to die. The next morning I was too ill to move. As yet, no one had taken my temperature.

The ship-to-shore radio went into action. Fortunately we had a Portuguese speaking man on board. This time the jolly boat arrived with the other doctor, a much younger man. He began by taking my temperature which was one hundred and four, then my blood pressure. I heard the word 'fever' uttered several times. Then El Grippe, then 'Hospital'. Here we go again. This time wrapped warmly in several blankets and heavily sedated I was back in the jolly boat heading for the beach, an ambulance was waiting, only this time it was stopped at the dock gates by the police who made a big pretence of searching the vehicle for contraband. Only when the Agent parted with a sum of Cruzeiros were we allowed to pass.

I was on my way to the Hospital Espaniol. There I remained lapsing in and out of fever for twenty three days. I was well treated at this Hospital which had a whole wing set aside for foreign seamen. One Greek Cypriot, obviously mentally ill, was demanding repatriation to fight the Turks!

When I was passed fit, I was given the option of flying home or returning to the ship which was now further South and was loading cargo at the little port of Rio Grande del Sol. I chose the latter.

I remained at sea for a further three years but the spring had gone from my step. No longer was I anxious to gallop down the gangway and go screaming ashore. Glasses were needed for reading. False teeth were required for eating. I hadn't saved a penny. There was no pension or golden handshake for seamen either. Could I, would I, readjust to living and working ashore? These thoughts and many more were being pondered.

We were homeward-bound, just north of the Equator. It was past midnight. My cabin was hot and humid. It was situated above the heat of the Engine Room. I had taken a pillow and blanket, and now lay prone out on the hatch. It was a beautiful, calm, sultry night. The ship rolled lazily on the shimmering moonlit South Atlantic. I gazed aloft at the distant stars. A spark winked as it escaped from the funnel.

If there was a heaven, surely this was it. I could feel a deep sense of contentment. My mind drifted back to the earlier days when I was aboard my first Deep Sea ship — the *Baron Renfrew*. I thought of the old bosun. I could hear his pipe tapping on the hatch coaming. His words came flooding back: 'Don't worry about the duration of voyages, Chippy, when you sign on, because your hand will be back on the Articles signing off just as quickly.'

Twenty-two years later I have to admit — he was right.